Contents

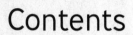

Introduction

ONCE YOU HIT rock bottom, you can only look up." That bit of wisdom came from a prisoner in Pennsylvania. Reading *An Anchor for the Soul* changed his life, and he wanted to let me know about it. Here's his story:

> Dear Ray Pritchard,
>   Hello, what's up? I hope you are doing okay. I have just read your book *An Anchor for the Soul*. I'm writing you because how I read it was an accident from God. It was the best thing that EVER happened to me in my life. Thanks to you I have found God.
>   I got into a fight and went into the

hole. So I was trading my food trays for envelopes (a kind of money in jail) and I wound up trading a food tray for a book to read. It's something to do because you're not allowed out of your cell. I looked at the book and thought, *Ah, a religious book; I got ripped off.* Cuz I never believed in God.

I decided to read the first little bit to see if I'd like it. Once I read that first prayer and everything before it, it touched me and I flew through the book. You covered every aspect I ever thought about. Thanks to you, I've found God. You're right, once you've hit rock bottom, you can only look up.

Thanks to your book and my accidentally stumbling upon it, I have a different outlook on life. The day I found God was 9/22/07. I think I'm going have it tattooed on my arm.

The man who wrote that letter came to Christ through an "accident from God." I love it when new believers talk about things and they don't use the vocabulary of people who've been inside the church a long time. They give God the glory for their salvation in their own unique language.

I also love the fact that he wasn't too excited when he "traded food trays and ended up with this book and wasn't too happy." He's not the first person to feel ripped off by religion. But I'm glad he started to read this book because it ended up changing his life.

When I wrote the first edition of this book ten years ago, I had no idea how God would use it. Over 500,000 copies have been printed since then. And we have received over 10,000 letters from readers who found my address in the back of the book. Many of them wrote to say God used this book to lead them to a personal relationship with Jesus Christ.

Maybe that will happen to you as you read this new edition of *An Anchor for the Soul*.

Everything in this book is based on two facts. First, you were made to know God, and you can't and won't be truly satisfied until you know Him personally. Second, the Bible tells us how we can know God personally. The Bible does not tell us everything we could know on every subject, but it tells us everything we need to know about being right with God. It only makes sense that the God who made us knows us better than we know ourselves. And we need to hear what He has to say. If you wonder about the title of this book,

it comes from Hebrews 6:19, "We have this hope as *an anchor for the soul*, firm and secure." When the waves of life threaten to overwhelm us, we need an anchor that will hold up in the strongest storm.

Let me say right up front that this book will be helpful no matter where you might be on your spiritual journey. When it comes to knowing God, we all stand in different places. Some are seekers, some are doubters, some are skeptics, and some know very little about the Christian faith. Others were raised in a church but drifted away years ago.

If you would like to know God, that's all that matters. You may count yourself as a religious person, or you may think of yourself as nonreligious. That's fine either way. Many people today have a deep interest in spiritual matters, even though they are not part of any religious organization. If that describes you, I hope you'll read this book carefully because I am writing to you as an individual in order to help you find a personal relationship with God.

I'm sure you have a few questions. I hope so, because honest questions deserve good answers. Here are some questions you may have:

⇨What is God like?
⇨How can I know Him?
⇨Am I really a sinner?
⇨How can my sins be forgiven?
⇨Who is Jesus, and what did He do?
⇨What does it mean to be a Christian?
⇨How can I find peace with God?
⇨How can I be sure I am going to heaven?

Maybe you are a bit skeptical about the whole concept of knowing God. Perhaps you've been turned off by organized religion or by certain Christians whose actions don't match up with what they say they believe. While I freely admit that Christians sometimes can be the worst advertisement for their faith, I hope you'll approach this book with an open mind.

I don't believe in trying to argue people into the Christian faith. If you are not inclined to believe in Jesus, nothing in this book will convince you to change your mind. The Bible says that no one comes to God unless the Father draws him through the Spirit (John 6:44). So if you're a skeptic, don't worry; you won't be converted against your will by reading this book.

On the other hand, this book could change

your life. If the gospel is truly good news from God, then we shouldn't be surprised if our lives are radically changed as we come to know God personally through the Lord Jesus Christ.

But I'm getting a bit ahead of myself. All we know so far is that this book contains good news that comes from God as revealed in the Bible. For the rest of the story, you'll need to read each chapter slowly and think about what it says. Before we start I'd like to suggest a simple prayer for spiritual guidance. I encourage you to read this prayer slowly, phrase by phrase. If it expresses the desire of your heart, pray it quietly to God.

> *O God, I want to know You.*
>
> *If You are really there, please reveal Yourself to me. Show me the truth about myself. Open my eyes and create faith in my heart. Give me the gift of an open mind to receive Your truth. Speak to me through what I read, that I may come to know You. Grant that my deepest questions may be answered with Your truth. Help me to seek You with all my heart. And may I find You and be satisfied with what I find. Amen.*

You shouldn't be fearful about praying a prayer like this because God never turns any honest seeker away. If you seek the Lord with all your heart you will find Him. You might want to put your initials and today's date by that prayer if it expresses the desire of your heart.

I encourage you not to rush through this book. I've included questions at the end of each chapter to help you go deeper. You'll gain much more if you take time to think about the questions and write out your answers. You'll also find great value in looking up the various Bible verses one by one. God invites us to seek Him with our whole heart. As you respond to what you learn, the Holy Spirit will be at work in you. So don't be surprised if you end up a different person when you are finished reading this book.

Now it's time to begin. The first step in knowing God is finding out more about who He really is.

Before you begin . . .

What questions would you like answered as you read this book?

Where are you on your spiritual journey right now?

1

A PLACE
to Begin

SUPPOSE I SAY TO YOU, "Define God in twenty words or less." And I give you thirty seconds to do it. What would you say? Could you do it? Does it seem unfair? Suppose I give you 200,000 words and thirty years. Would it be any easier? And would you come any closer to the truth?

Since God is the ultimate source of all reality, we can't really "define" Him. But we can say this: *Knowing God is the most important thing in life.* If you live thirty or forty or fifty or sixty or seventy or eighty years and you don't know God, then it doesn't matter what else you have done with your life. If you don't know God, you have missed the very reason

for your existence. When we put God at the center of all things, then everything else finds its proper place. "The fear of the Lord is the beginning of wisdom, and knowledge of the Holy One is insight" (Proverbs 9:10). If you want wisdom, know God! If you want knowledge, seek the Lord!

If you miss out on knowing God, you have missed the central reality of the universe. Compared to knowing the One who made you, everything else is just crumbs and nibbling around the edges.

Our Need—
To Know the God Who Made Us

We were made to know God, and something inside every one of us desperately wants to know Him. We are incurably religious by nature. That's why every human society—no matter how primitive—has some concept of a higher power, some vision of a reality that goes beyond the natural. On one level, that explains why science has not eliminated religion from the earth. Science can never do that because technological achievement can't meet the deepest needs of the human heart.

We want to know the answers to the three most basic questions of life: Where did I come

from? Why am I here? Where am I going? And we will spend money, buy books, watch videos, attend seminars, search the Internet, and travel great distances to find the answers. A book claiming to report one woman's after-death visit to heaven climbed to the top of the best-seller list. There are even TV programs featuring mediums who claim to be able to contact dead family members. People are hungry for spiritual truth, and they will reach for anyone or anything that claims to give them an answer.

It is the same in every country and every culture. On the surface we are very different in our appearance, background, language, and customs. But dig a little deeper and you discover that basically, we are all the same. Look beneath the surface and you discover no real difference between a person born in poverty in Haiti and a corporate lawyer on Wall Street; or between a schoolteacher in Addis Ababa, Ethiopia, and a computer scientist in Singapore. Everywhere we are the same—with the same longings, regrets, dreams, and hopes; with the same need to love and be loved; with the same desire to be remembered after we die; and with the same sense that there must be a God of some kind who made us.

We were made to know God, and we need to know Him. God designed us so that we would want to know Him—and then He guaranteed we wouldn't be happy unless He Himself fills the emptiness within. This brings us face-to-face with the famous statement that there is a "God-shaped vacuum" inside each person. We can turn to God, or we can fill the vacuum with idols of our own making or the evil spirits of our ancestors. Something in us drives us to seek ultimate meaning. That "something" is put there by God. Augustine, an ancient Christian theologian, gave us this frequently heard prayer: "You have made us for Yourself, and our hearts are restless until they find their rest in You."

God's Desire— That We Should Know Him

The whole Bible demonstrates that God wants us to know Him. In a sense, that is the theme of the Bible—how God loved us, how we rebelled against Him, and how God set about rescuing people who had turned against Him. The story is clear enough. God sent prophets, priests, and messengers of various sorts. He sent His messages in writing. But we (all the people on earth) didn't want anything

P9-CFE-541

The gospel is "the" good news in a bad news world. What is it? Ray Pritchard answers that question in a way that will not only define it, but lead you to delight in it.

—DR. JOSEPH M. STOWELL, president,
 Cornerstone University

With great clarity, Dr. Pritchard provides an illuminating explanation of the supreme, sublime truths of the universe, and God's great plan. This is absolutely compelling, and life-changing.

—BILL BRIGHT, founder,
 Campus Crusade for Christ International

A wonderful summary of what the Christian faith is all about. Ray Pritchard presents the gospel of Jesus Christ not as an idea to be studied but as an urgent message to be received and responded to. This is a compelling account of the Savior's love.

—TIMOTHY GEORGE, dean,
 Beeson Divinity School

Simple and straightforward, clear and concise. This book cuts through any confusion and showcases what the gospel of Jesus Christ is all about. It reads easy, but runs deep!

—JONI EARECKSON TADA,
 author and artist

In memory of
Gary Olson
He loved to tell the story.
How beautiful upon the mountains are the feet
of him who brings good news.
Isaiah 52:7 NKJV

© 2000, 2011 by
RAY PRITCHARD

All rights reserved. No part of this book may be reproduced in any form without permission in writing from the publisher, except in the case of brief quotations embodied in critical articles or reviews.

All Scripture quotations, unless otherwise indicated, are taken from the *Holy Bible, New International Version*®. NIV®. Copyright © 1973, 1978, 1984 by Biblica, Inc.™. Used by permission of Zondervan. All rights reserved worldwide.

Scripture quotations marked NASB are taken from the *New American Standard Bible*®, © Copyright The Lockman Foundation 1960, 1962, 1963, 1968, 1971, 1972, 1973, 1975, 1977, 1995. Used by permission.

Scripture quotations marked NKJV are taken from the *New King James Version*. Copyright © 1982 by Thomas Nelson, Inc. Used by permission. All rights reserved.

Scripture quotations marked ESV are taken from the *Holy Bible, English Standard Version*. Copyright © 2000, 2001 by Crossway Bibles, a division of Good News Publishers. Used by permission. All rights reserved.

Scripture quotations marked NLT are taken from *The Holy Bible, New Living Translation*, copyright © 1996, 2004. Used by permission of Tyndale House Publishers, Inc., Wheaton, Illinois 60189, U.S.A. All rights reserved.

Scripture quotations marked CEV are taken from the *Contemporary English Version*. Copyright © 1991, 1992, 1995 by American Bible Society. Used by permission.

Scriptures quoted marked NCV are from the *Holy Bible, New Century Version*, copyright © 1987, 1988, 1991 by Word Publishing, Nashville, TN 37214. Used by permission.

Scripture quotations marked KJV are taken from the King James Version.

Interior design: Ragont Design
Cover design: Tan Nguyen
Cover image: Getty and iStock

Library of Congress Cataloging-in-Publication Data

Pritchard, Ray
  An anchor for the soul : help for the present, hope for the future / Ray Pritchard.
    p. cm.
  ISBN 978-0-8024-1536-3
  1. Theology, Doctrinal—Popular works. I. Title.
  BT77.P74 2011
  230--dc22

                          2010028261

We hope you enjoy this book from Moody Publishers. Our goal is to provide high-quality, thought-provoking books and products that connect truth to your real needs and challenges. For more information on other books and products written and produced from a biblical perspective, go to www.moodypublishers.com or write to:

Moody Publishers
820 N. LaSalle Boulevard
Chicago, IL 60610

7 9 10 8

Printed in the United States of America

RAY PRITCHARD

An
ANCHOR for
the SOUL

HELP for the Present,
HOPE for the Future

Moody Publishers
CHICAGO

to do with God. So we ignored His message and sometimes killed His messengers. Then He sent His Son, Jesus Christ, the ultimate expression of His love. And we killed Him, too. But through His death God made a way for each and every one of us to be forgiven.

Let's go back to the very beginning of the story for a moment. When God first created the world, He created Adam and Eve and made them "in his image" and "after his likeness." "So God created man in his own image, in the image of God he created him; male and female he created them" (Genesis 1:27). These simple phrases are full of meaning for us. We were made in God's image, which means there is something in us that corresponds to who God is. You and I were designed to know God personally. Dogs don't pray, birds don't worship, fish don't praise—but we do. Why? Because there is an awareness of God inside every human heart. It is this "God-consciousness" that makes us want to know God and makes us eager to find out why we exist.

Father Hunger

But there's another part of the story. Ever since Adam and Eve sinned in the garden of Eden, that image of God within each of us has been distorted by sin. I picture a piece of paper with the words GOD'S IMAGE in huge letters. Before Adam and Eve sinned, that paper was clean and smooth. Now for all of us that paper is crumpled, dirty, and torn. But it is never completely destroyed. Despite all our failures, we still want to know God, and we still want to find meaning in life but just don't know where to look.

To use a very modern phrase, we are left with a kind of "Father hunger." That's a phrase used to describe children growing up in a family without a strong and loving father figure. He may have died or he may have abandoned his family. Or perhaps he was so busy he had no time for his family. Because he barely knows his children, they compete desperately for his little scraps of love and approval. Children growing up in a home like this desperately want a father, and sometimes they will look for someone (or something) to fill that void.

On a much larger scale, that's the story of all humanity. We were made to know God and we want to know Him, but our sin has separated us from God. As a result, we are left with a deep "Father hunger" that won't go away.

Our Search—
in All the Wrong Places

So what do we do? We look for love in all the wrong places. We can illustrate this using a pen and a piece of paper. Draw a cliff on the right side of the paper and label it "God." On the left side draw another cliff and label it "Us." Label the gap in between with the word "Sin." That's the problem we all face. We're on one side, God is on the other, and our sin stands between God and us. Something deep inside tells us we belong on the other side with the God who made us. So we set out to build bridges across the great chasm.

Now draw lines that start on the "Us" side and move toward the "God" side, ending each line somewhere in-between the two cliffs. Each line represents a human "bridge" we build in our attempts to find our way back to God. One bridge is labeled "Money," another "Education," another "Good works," another "Sex," another "Power," another "Science," another "Success," another "Approval," another "Relationships," and another "Religion." You can make as many bridges as you like, but they never seem to reach the other side. Each one ends somewhere in the middle, illustrating the truth that you can never find God by starting where you are. No matter which road you take, you fall into the great chasm and end up being broken on the jagged rocks of reality.

That's what I mean by searching in all the wrong places. Nothing in this world can satisfy our longing because nothing in this world can lead us back to God. The answer we need must come from outside this world.

Three thousand years ago, a wise man named Solomon went on a search to find the key to the meaning of life. He recorded his findings in a book of the Bible called Ecclesiastes. In the first two chapters he tells about his grand experiment. He built buildings, planted vast gardens, tried the party scene, and built up a vast fortune. He gathered books and a great deal of human knowledge. Anything he wanted, he got for himself. Nothing was held back. He tried anything and everything in his search for meaning.

He reported his finding in three terse words: **"I hated life"** (Ecclesiastes 2:17). When nothing satisfies, when you've truly tried it all, when you can say with calm assurance, "Been there, done that" and you still feel the emptiness within, what do you do then? Solomon's conclusion could stand as an epitaph for every generation.

Here is our problem in a nutshell. We were made by God to know God. There is a "God-shaped vacuum" inside each person that causes us to seek after the One who made us. Solomon reminds us in Ecclesiastes 3:11 that God "has put eternity in their hearts." Because we search in all the wrong places, we can never find Him. Our eternal longing for God is not fulfilled.

God's Solution— He Has Made Himself Known

In the end we are left with this great truth: We can never know God unless He reveals Himself to us. Try as we might we always end up in the darkness, seeking a God we know is there but cannot seem to find. But God has not left us to live in darkness forever. He has revealed Himself in four primary ways:

A. In creation—Everyone sees this.
B. In the human conscience—Everyone has this.
C. In His written Word, the Bible—Not everyone knows this.
D. In His Son, Jesus Christ—Not everyone understands this.

The last revelation is the most important. Jesus is "God incarnate," that is, God clothed with human flesh. When Jesus walked on the earth, He was the God-man, fully God and fully man at the same time. Jesus is the supreme revelation of God. Jesus said, "Anyone who has seen me has seen the Father" (John 14:9). Jesus is the key to knowing God. If you want to know what God is like, look at Jesus.

Some Facts about God

The Bible says a great deal about who God is and how He has revealed Himself. Here are six facts about God you need to know:

1. *He eternally exists in three persons*

The truth about God begins with the fact that He always exists as the Father, the Son, and the Holy Spirit. When we say that, we mean that the Father is God, the Son is God, and the Holy Spirit is God, but they are not three gods but only one God. The Father is not the Son, the Son is not the Spirit, the Spirit is not the Father, but each is God individually and yet they are together the one true God of the Bible. This is called the doctrine of the Holy Trinity.

Someone asked American statesman

Daniel Webster, "How can a man of your intellect believe in the Trinity?" "I do not pretend fully to understand the arithmetic of heaven now," he replied. That's a good phrase—the arithmetic of heaven.

The Trinity should cause us to bow in humility before a God who is greater than our minds could ever comprehend. We have a God who has provided everything necessary for our salvation. When we were lost in sin, our God acted in every person of His being to save us. The Father gave the Son, the Son offered Himself on the cross, and the Holy Spirit draws us to Jesus.

2. *He is the Sovereign Lord*

To call God "sovereign" means that He is the Ultimate Ruler of the universe. There is no one higher than He is. He answers to no one but everyone must one day answer to him. God is the purest, simplest, most basic being in the universe. He is a personal God—not an impersonal force. Because He is infinite, He is not subject to time, corruption, or decay. Because He is eternal, He is always present everywhere in the universe. He is the "unmoved mover," "the uncaused first cause," and the source of all that is. He is the power behind all other power.

His character is unchanging—and therefore entirely dependable. What He says, He will do. Because He has the only truly "free will" in the universe, He does whatever He pleases, yet He never acts in an arbitrary fashion, but only in conformity with His own perfect character. "Our God is in heaven; he does whatever pleases him" (Psalm 115:3).

God is holy, which means He is utterly pure, free from all evil, totally without blame or error. Holiness is what makes God God. He never lowers His standards, never compromises, and makes no "deals." All that He does is right, just, and good. "He is the Rock, his works are perfect, and all his ways are just" (Deuteronomy 32:4). There is no falsehood in Him or from Him. He makes the rules, and no one can object. He Himself is the final standard of right and wrong. Therefore, everything He says about you and me is true.

3. *He created all things*

God designed everything that is; He initiated creation and personally brought all things into being. "In the beginning God created the heavens and the earth" (Genesis 1:1). The universe did not happen by chance, accident, or by the random collision of cells. It is not the product of random evolution. God spoke and the universe came into being. He is so powerful that He is the source of all things—living and nonliving. All things were made by Him, and all things exist at this moment by His powerful word (Hebrews 11:3). This means that He personally created you, that you were put on this earth for a reason, and that the highest purpose of your life is to know the God who made you. Think about that for a moment. The God who can create anything—created you! And He wants you to know Him personally.

4. *He made you in His image*

You were made to know God. Something in you truly wants to know the God who created you. That desire may be hidden deep within, or you may feel it burning inside you at this moment. Perhaps you have tried to cover it up or to satisfy your longings with the things of this world. But that doesn't work. You were made with desires that nothing in this world can satisfy. Only God can fill the hole in your heart. Only God can love you the way you long to be loved.

5. *He knows all about you*

Theologians call this "omniscience," which simply means that God knows everything—the past, the present, and the future. He is never caught by surprise by anything that happens anywhere in the universe. Nothing is hidden from Him. That includes your secret thoughts, your dreams, and your unfulfilled desires. He knows your words before you speak them and your thoughts before you think them. "Before a word is on my tongue you know it completely, O Lord" (Psalm 139:4). He knows where you were last night and who you were with. He knows the whole story of your life—the good, the bad, and the ugly. What about those secret things that no one else knows about? He knows them all, and He knows them completely.

6. *He cares about you*

The Bible tells us that "God is love" (1 John 4:16). He is perfect, infinite, unconditional love. His love is freely given. It is not a reward for good behavior because no one can ever "earn" God's love. The greatest gifts in life are the ones we don't deserve. No gift could be greater than the love of God. The Bible declares that God loves the unlovely. We shook our fists at God and sinned against Him. The amazing news is that God even loves His enemies (Romans 5:6–8). While we were sinners, God demonstrated His love by sending His Son to the earth to die for us.

We need to know a God who loves us like that. To miss knowing this God is to miss the central truth of the universe. It's like visiting Rome and seeing everything but St. Peter's Square. It's like traveling to Washington, D.C., and seeing everything but the White House. It's like going to Paris and seeing everything but the Eiffel Tower. Or it's like going to the Super Bowl and watching everything but the football game.

The Only Thing that Matters Is God

Let's wrap up this chapter with a story about a young man I knew who was only twenty-six years old when he died. Although he grew up in a Christian home, during his teens and early twenties he went through a period of rebellion and spiritual searching. His life changed when the doctors discovered a brain tumor. Surgery brought a brief remission, but then the cancer returned.

As the months passed, his faith increased

even as his physical condition worsened. He began to seek the Lord as never before. The Word of God became sweet to him. He became very bold in sharing what God had done in his life, especially to his many friends. He asked God to use him to reach others so that he could point people to Christ, no matter how long he lived.

During the funeral, his younger sister talked about how much she loved him, how as a young girl she wanted to be like him, and how annoying he could be at times. Then the cancer came. She saw a difference so profound that it changed everything. Her brother had figured out what life is all about. Then she said this sentence: *Life is nothing without God.* He had shown her that it doesn't matter how long you live or how much money you have or even how well you do in your career. His faith at the end spoke one simple message: Life is nothing without God. She marveled that someone so young—her brother—had figured out the meaning of life. And she thanked him for leaving her with that all-important truth: Life is nothing without God.

When I stood up to deliver the message a few minutes later, I didn't have to say very much. I simply repeated what she said one more time: Life is nothing without God.

I then made this application. If you live for eighty years but don't discover that truth, you've missed the very reason for your own existence. If you should earn a million dollars—or $10 million—and have hundreds of friends and the praise of your closest friends, if you have all that but don't figure out this basic truth, you're still in spiritual kindergarten.

Have you discovered what life is all about? Life is nothing without God. Everything else is just details. Knowing the God who made you is the most important thing in life. It gives meaning and purpose to everything else. If you don't know God, nothing else matters.

So the question we need to ask is this: Do you know God, and if you don't, would you like to know Him? The good news is, you can know Him. But before we can get to the good news, we have to face the bad news. And that's what the next chapter is all about.

A TRUTH TO REMEMBER

If you live for eighty years but don't know the God who created you, you've missed the very reason for your own existence.

Going Deeper

Which of the following best describes where you are on your spiritual journey right now?

_____Seeker

_____Honest Doubter

_____Frustrated Skeptic

_____True Believer

_____Casual Onlooker

_____Spiritual but Not Religious

_____Former Believer

_____Mostly Confused

_____Hopelessly Lost

Read Jeremiah 29:11. What does this verse tell us about the importance of seeking God?

Which is harder for you to believe—that God loves you and wants a relationship with you or that God will someday judge you because of your sins?

What do these Old Testament passages tell us about who God is?

Exodus 34:5–7

Psalm 103:8–13

Isaiah 6:1–3

Daniel 4:34–37

2

THE TRUTH
about You

A FEW YEARS AGO a friend passed along a clipping from a Chicago newspaper regarding an odd bit of information tucked away in the obituaries. It seems that "Wally the Wiretapper" had died. Normally that wouldn't rate any special attention, but as I read the clipping, I realized that "Wally the Wiretapper" was no ordinary crook.

The obituary called him a "fabled Chicago felon" who engaged in a "variety of crime as a Damon Runyon-like character." He freely admitted to tapping phones for his clients, who included various well-known mobsters. He evidently was good at what he did. During his criminal career, he had been convicted of, among other things, defrauding insurance companies; posing as a federal agent; and past-posting horse races, which means he used electronic equipment to place bets on races that had already been run in other cities.

At one point in his long career, he was approached by certain Hollywood types who wanted to make a movie about his life. But he was persuaded not to go along when his friends in the mob gently discussed the matter with him. "My friends in the mob," he said, "asked how I was going to spend the movie profits if I was six feet down. I got the message, and I said good-bye to the Hollywood screenwriter."

I was attracted to his story when I learned his real name—Walter Dewey Pritchard. When Mr. Pritchard was sentenced in 1984 after being convicted of interstate racketeering, the presiding judge made a telling comment. "I see no redeeming features for Mr. Pritchard at all, except that he's a nice guy." It made me wonder if Wally and I don't share the same family tree. As far as I know there is no direct connection, but I'll bet if you go back far enough, you would discover that he's really my uncle, four times removed.

That wasn't the end of my reflection. As

I pondered the matter, I realized that story could have been written about me. "Uncle" Wally and I have more in common than I would like to admit. A little more reflection led me to an unnerving conclusion: What the judge said about Wally the Wiretapper, he could have said about me: "I see no redeeming features for Mr. Pritchard at all, except that he's a nice guy." From a biblical standpoint, that's a perfectly accurate statement. There are no redeeming features in me.

Whatever Became of Sin?

If you think this is overly harsh, consider the words of British author G. K. Chesterton: "Whatever else is or is not true, this one thing is certain—man is not what he was meant to be." I'm sure I don't need to spend a great deal of time debating that point. If you have any question about how sinful we are, go anywhere in the world and pick up any newspaper you want, in any language. Simply read the front page and you will be convinced.

In 1973 psychiatrist Karl Menninger wrote a landmark book, *Whatever Became of Sin?* There are many answers to that question, but this one is certainly true: Nothing has happened to sin, but something has happened to us. We simply don't want to talk about sin anymore. It isn't a polite topic, especially not in polite society. Try mentioning the word "sin" the next time you go to a party and see how quickly the subject is changed.

But avoiding the subject doesn't change the truth. Something has gone wrong with the human race. No one can deny that fact. We are not all that we could be. And no matter how much we boast of our technological achievements, the fact of man's inhumanity to man always grabs the front page. The details change, the faces come and go, but the story is always the same. Something evil lurks inside the heart of every person. No one is immune, no one is exempt, and no one is truly innocent.

Call it what you will—a twist, an inclination, a desire to do wrong. Somehow, somewhere, someone injected poison into the human bloodstream. That's why, even when we know the right thing to do, we often choose to do what is wrong. Deliberately. Repeatedly. Defiantly.

The world is a mess—we all know that. The world is a mess because we ourselves are messed up. The problem is not "out there." It's "in us." The world is bad because we are bad. The world is evil because evil lurks within us.

Don't Forget to Lock Your Car

It is common today to talk about evil as a result of a bad environment, lack of education, or poverty. Many people believe that if we could change those things, we could wipe out evil in the world. We hope to change people by changing their environment. After billions and billions of dollars, it hasn't happened, and it won't happen. Today we have produced a generation of cyber-criminals who use the Internet to commit crime from thousands of miles away. Through modern technology we know how to kill more people with less effort than ever before. Racism remains, killing continues, crime spreads, and nations are still at war. Ethnic violence seems to be the order of the day. Why? Because there is evil inside the human heart.

During a sermon I asked how many people locked the doors to their homes and cars before coming inside the church. The answer was, almost everyone. We have elaborate security systems because human nature has not been improved.

Our problem is sin that separates us from God. "Your sins are the roadblock between you and your God" (Isaiah 59:2 CEV). We call it by other names, whitewash it, and then relabel it. But it doesn't work. You can take a bottle of rat poison and label it Orange Juice but that doesn't change its basic character. If you drink it, you will die. Poison is still poison, no matter what you call it.

The Nature of Sin

What is sin? It is any violation of God's righteous character. It is anything we say or do or think or imagine or plan that does not meet God's standard of perfection. The Bible uses many word pictures to describe sin:

Sin is *lawlessness*. That means sin is anything that ignores or violates the standard God laid down in the Bible.

Sin is *missing the mark*. Picture an archer shooting an arrow and missing so badly that not only does he not hit the bull's-eye, he doesn't even hit anywhere on the target. Sin causes us to aim our lives in the wrong direction and to miss the mark of what God wants us to do and to be.

Sin is *transgression*. This means going beyond the limits of what God has said is good and proper.

Sin is *iniquity*. This is a stronger word that means deliberately choosing to do wrong. It

has within it the idea of premeditated disobedience.

Sin is *deviation from the standard*. This
describes a crookedness of the soul that results
in a life full of twisted choices, evil deeds, and
broken relationships.

Sin *touches the inner ugliness of the soul*. It
involves our thoughts, our dreams, and our
hidden motivations that no one can see. But
God sees everything. So much takes place
beneath the surface. We can hide from others,
and even hide from ourselves, but we cannot
hide from God. All things are laid bare before
His all-seeing eyes (Hebrews 4:13).

The Bible traces sin back to the garden of
Eden. God told Adam and Eve not to eat of
the fruit of one particular tree. The serpent
deceived Eve, who ate the fruit and then
offered some to Adam who, though he was
not deceived, ate the fruit anyway. It was
through that deliberate choice that sin entered
the world. Before that moment he was a living
soul in an immortal body. After that moment
he was a dead soul in a dying body. If you had
been there that day, all you would have seen
was a man taking fruit from his wife and eating
it. No lightning, no thunder, no bells, no scary
music in the background. Yet from that one act

of disobedience, disastrous results flowed out across history.

Theologians call this event "The Fall." It means that when Adam ate the fruit he fell from a state of innocence into a state of guilt. He fell from grace to judgment. He fell from life to death.

Adam Drove
the Bus off the Cliff

What does all this have to do with you and me? In some mysterious way, you and I were there. When Adam sinned, you sinned with him and so did I. "Sin entered the world through one man, and death through sin, and in this way death came to all men, because all sinned" (Romans 5:12). This is the doctrine of original sin in its plainest form. It means that when Adam sinned, you and I sinned. When Adam disobeyed, you and I disobeyed. When Adam fell, you and I fell. When he died, you and I died. To say it another way, although we were not historically there in the garden, because we are descendants of Adam— part of his family tree—we suffer the consequences of what he did.

Let me say it another way. Adam was the driver of the bus of humanity. When he drove the bus over the cliff, we went down with him. Or you could say he was at the controls when the plane crashed. It doesn't matter that we were back in the coach section watching a movie. When he crashed, we all went up in flames.

When Adam sinned, he tainted the human bloodstream. The virus of sin entered the human bloodstream, and as a result, every baby born into this world is tainted with the deadly sin virus. Every person is born with a tendency to do wrong. We're all born with a sin nature.

We may not like to face this truth about ourselves, and we may protest that we had nothing to do with Adam's sin. A friend told me that his father has a painful disease called gout and three of the sons also have gout. He said his father often jokingly remarked to his boys, "You didn't choose your parents very well." But we don't choose our parents—physically or spiritually. We had nothing to do with the physical characteristics we inherited from our parents. Likewise, we inherited a sin nature from Adam because he is at the root of every family tree in the whole human race.

Many people think God has some kind of divine meter that registers "Good," "Neutral," and "Evil." They think that they are some-where right in the middle—not too bad, not too good, mostly just neutral. They aren't the best, but they aren't the worst either. But the Bible tells us that because of Adam's sin we come into the world with the needle stuck firmly on "Evil." Apart from the grace of God, that's where the needle will stay as long as we live.

You're not evil because you do evil. You do evil because you are evil. Your basic nature is corrupt and wicked. That's your inheritance from Adam. You are born living on the Wild Side. You are born with a minus on your record. You turned the wrong way back in the garden and you've been going the wrong way ever since.

It started with Adam, but it didn't end there. It continues in your life and in mine. Adam was the first sinner, but he wasn't the last. We follow in the footsteps of our fore-father because we share his tainted blood.

If Sin Were Blue

I can imagine someone reading to this point and saying, "Don't you have any good news to share? Is there any hope?" The answer is yes, there is enormous hope for all of us.

The good news is coming, but we're not quite ready to hear it yet. We need to understand the depth of our problem before we can fully appreciate the wonder of God's solution.

How bad is the problem? Here is the bottom line: Sin has infected every part of your being—your mind, your emotions, your will, your intellect, your moral reasoning, your decision making, your words, and your deeds. No part of your life is exempt from the debilitating effects of sin. As someone has said, "If sin were blue, we'd be blue all over." Part would be dark blue, part would be sky blue, part would be light blue, but every part would be blue in one shade or another.

This leaves us with God's solemn statement that "there is no one righteous, not even one" (Romans 3:10). As God looks down from heaven, He doesn't see a single righteous person—not even one. But how can this be? How can God look down at over 6 billion people and not see even one person whose life pleases Him? Is this not an overly harsh judgment? The answer is that God judges according to a different standard from the one we use. Most of us grade on the curve. That is, we look to our neighbor and say, "I'm not as bad as he is." Or we compare ourselves with someone we know at work who makes us look good, or so we think.

But God doesn't judge that way. When He looks down from heaven, the standard He uses is His own sinless perfection. He compares us to His own perfect holiness, His own perfect love, His own perfect wisdom, and His own perfect justice. Compared with God's perfection, there is no one—not even one person—who is righteous in His eyes.

Looking for a Righteous Person

Where, then, will you find a righteous person on the earth? In Brazil? No. In Afghanistan? No. In Japan? No. In South Africa? No. In Turkey? No. In Israel? No. In America? No. Will you find a righteous person in Congress? No. How about Hollywood? Forget it. Can you find a righteous person in the churches? Not a chance. Is there anywhere in all the earth where we could find a truly righteous man or woman? The answer is no. From God's point of view there isn't a single righteous person in the entire human race.

Even as we read these words, there is something in us that resists this harsh conclusion. When God looks down from heaven,

He sees a race of people who are sinful through and through. We are like a basket of fruit that has gone rotten in the hot summer sun. We have all "gone bad" in the eyes of God.

Since we all descend from Adam, there is no room for pride or a feeling of superiority over others. We all stand in exactly the same place—created by God, made to know Him, deeply fallen, and greatly loved. And we all need the saving touch of Jesus Christ.

Part of our problem at this point is that it's easy for us to confess someone else's sins. The tendency toward hypocrisy shows itself in many subtle ways. Have you ever noticed how we like to "rename" our sins? We do that by assigning the worst motives to others, while using other phrases to let ourselves off the hook. If you do it, you're a liar; if I do it, I merely "stretch the truth." If you do it, you're cheating; if I do it, I am "bending the rules."

⇨ You lose your temper; I have righteous anger.

⇨ You're a jerk; I'm having a bad day.

⇨ You curse and swear; I let off steam.

⇨ You're pushy; I'm intensely goal oriented.

⇨ You're greedy; I'm simply taking care of business.

⇨ You're a hypochondriac; but I'm really sick.

⇨ You stink; I merely have an "earthy aroma."

And so it goes. We all have a thousand ways to excuse our own behavior while at the same time criticizing others for doing the same things. No wonder Jesus said, "Let the one who has never sinned throw the first stone!" (John 8:7 NLT). If we all followed that standard, the volume of criticism in the world would rapidly fall to zero.

A good friend was having trouble in his marriage. When I asked him what was his main problem and what was her main problem, my friend smiled ruefully and said with total honesty, "I see her problems much better than I see my own." I smiled and admitted that I'm the same way. I always look pretty good to myself. That's human nature, isn't it? All of us, even the best of us, are prone to hypocrisy because we all by nature let ourselves off the hook too easily. And when the excuse making is finally over, we come back to where we started. We are all sinners.

Your position in life doesn't change the

reality of your condition before God. You may be a...

> student
> career employee
> corporate executive
> stay-at-home mom or dad
> single parent
> senior adult
> man of means
> woman of wealth
> good citizen
> innocent man wrongly convicted

It doesn't matter. You are still a sinner in the eyes of God.

The Consequences of Sin

Where does all this leave us? We can sum up the biblical data this way. Because of sin we are . . .

- *Lost*—To be lost means to be in a position of great personal danger because you cannot find your way to safety.
- *Separated from God*—Sin has created a great chasm between God and us. We were made to know God, but our sin keeps us from

Him. We feel it, and we know it is true. There is a thick wall between us, a mountain of sin rising up, and a deep valley beneath us. This is why we are restless. Nothing on earth can satisfy our hunger for God. This is why we are seeking and searching and trying and striving.

- *Blind*—Sin destroys our ability to see things clearly. We live in the darkness of sin, and not even the tiniest ray of light breaks through to us.

- *Dead*—A dead person has eyes but cannot see, ears but cannot hear, lips but cannot speak, feet but cannot move. The spiritually dead have within them no ability to respond to God. Unless someone raises them to life, they can never know the God who made them.

- *Enslaved*—Because of sin we are slaves to our own evil desires. Even our hearts have been corrupted. Left to ourselves, we repeatedly choose to do wrong. Try as we might we cannot change ourselves. We are enslaved, and we cannot set ourselves free! God says, "Thou shalt not"; but we say, "I shall," and then we hate ourselves afterward. Why? We are enslaved to sin. Sin masters us, rules us, dominates us. We are a people of high ideals

52

and weak wills, of big dreams and small deeds, of high hopes and low living.

* *Helpless*—This is the logical end of it all. A person who is lost, separated, blind, dead, and enslaved is truly helpless. He is trapped with no hope. Any help must come from somewhere else.

The First Step Is the Hardest

Not long ago a man wrote to tell me about a ministry he and his wife share. Their goal is to help anyone struggling with issues of alcohol addiction. The man commented that for most alcoholics (he was speaking from personal experience) the hardest part of the process is admitting that you need help. He spoke of the difficulty of being totally honest about the mess your life is in and how easy it is to rationalize, to minimize, to make excuses, to tell part of the truth but not all the truth. Those who have been in the program will tell you that the first step is the hardest—and the most crucial. Until you face the bad news about your condition, you can't truly and totally turn your life over to God and ask for His help.

The same is true for all of us, no matter

what our personal issues might be. Sin has left us powerless and enslaved, totally unable to save ourselves. Until we admit this, our lives can never really change.

It's entirely possible that you don't see your life in those terms. To say that you are a sinner doesn't mean you are as bad as you could possibly be. Few of us ever reach the lowest depths of our own sinful inclinations. But if we are honest, we must admit that even on our best days, we fall far short of God's standard of absolute perfection. Even if your life seems to be in good shape, the Bible says that you are still a sinner. This is God's verdict on the whole human race.

Here is the bottom line: You were born in sin—separated from God, fallen, corrupt, spiritually dead. You are dying physically and are already dead spiritually. You are responsible for every sin you have ever committed.

You are in big trouble. Unless Someone intervenes to help you, you can never be saved.

#1 in Open-heart Surgery

I have several good friends who have gone through very difficult chemotherapy treatments for cancer. For some it was a very unpleasant experience indeed. I know of no one who takes chemotherapy for the fun of it. You take it because the doctor says, "If you don't, you will die." So you take it as the only available remedy. If sin is the cancer of the soul, then the gospel is God's divine remedy. In fact, it is the only remedy for sin.

A friend told me about a billboard posted near a Chicago expressway advertising the cardiac services of Christ Hospital in the Oak Lawn area. The billboard reads: "Christ is #1 in Open-heart Surgeries." I don't know about the hospital, but I can vouch for its namesake. Jesus Christ is indeed #1 in open-heart surgery. He has never lost a case yet. When you come to Him by faith, He gives you a brand-new heart.

The gospel is good news. But until we see how bad the bad news is, we will never understand why the good news is so good.

If you are still reading this, take heart! The worst is over. Good news is just around the corner.

A TRUTH TO REMEMBER

The only people who think they are good enough to go to heaven are the people who don't know how bad they really are.

Going Deeper

1. Do you consider yourself a sinner? Why or why not? How do you define "sin"?

2. Do you believe in heaven and hell? Why or why not? How certain are you about this? If you died right now where would you go: heaven, hell, or somewhere else? How important is it to you to know the answer to the last question?

3. What do the following verses teach about our true condition apart from God's grace?

   Luke 19:10 We are _____.

   Ephesians 2:1–2 We are spiritually _____.

Isaiah 59:2 We are _____ from God.

Titus 3:3 We are _____ to sin.

2 Corinthians 4:4 We are spiritually _____.

John 3:18 We are _____ already.

In light of these verses, how would you answer someone who says, "I may be a sinner but I'm not that bad off. I can handle my problems on my own"?

For each of the following statements, write "Agree" or "Do not agree" or "Not sure."

_____ God is very angry with me because of my sin.

_____ Everything is fine between me and God.

_____ God knows I'm doing the best I can right now.

_____ I'm not perfect but I wouldn't call myself a sinner.

_____ Most of my problems are not really my fault.

_____ If I'm good enough, God will forgive my sins.

_____ I don't worry about God and He doesn't worry about me.

_____ God loves me in spite of my sin.

_____ I don't believe in the concept of sin.

_____ I'm a sinner! There's no question about that.

3

AMAZING
Grace

IN HIS BOOK *What's So Amazing About Grace?* Philip Yancey comments that grace is the "last great word." He means that it is one of the last of the old English words that has retained something of its original meaning: "free and undeserved bounty." He points out that when we pray, we "say grace" to thank God for our food. We are "grateful" for a kindness shown by another person. To show our thanks we offer a "gratuity." Something that is offered at no cost is said to be "gratis." And when we have overdue books from the library, we may return them at no charge during a "grace period."

It is commonly said that Christianity is

supremely a religion of grace. And that is certainly true. We sing about grace, we write poems about grace, we name our churches and our children after grace. But for all that, grace is not well understood and often not really believed. We use the word a great deal but rarely think about what it means. Part of our problem is in the nature of grace itself. Grace is scandalous. Hard to accept. Hard to believe. Hard to receive. We all have a certain skepticism when a telemarketer tells us, "I'm not trying to sell you anything. I just want to offer you a free trip to Hawaii." Automatically we wonder, "What's the catch?" because we have all been taught that there's no free lunch.

Yancey points out that grace shocks us in what it offers. It is truly not of this world. It frightens us because of what it does for sinners. Grace teaches us that God does for others what we would never do for them. Grace is a gift that costs everything to the giver and nothing to the receiver. It is given to those who don't deserve it, barely recognize it, and hardly appreciate it.

Jeffrey Dahmer and Me

As I pondered Yancey's words, I recalled an illustration I read not long ago. It goes something like this. Consider for a moment the deeds of Jeffrey Dahmer, the notorious serial murderer. After he was arrested and imprisoned, he professed faith in Jesus Christ. That is, he claimed to have seen the error of his ways, confessed his sins, and cried out to Jesus for forgiveness. We'll never know the full story of what happened because he was beaten to death in prison not long after that.

When we think about Jeffrey Dahmer and the possibility that he might truly have been saved after those heinous crimes, our first response may be to say, "There is grace *even* for people like Jeffrey Dahmer." That statement, true as it is, reveals at least as much about us as it does about him. Think about that word "even." We admit that God would save "even" a man like Jeffrey Dahmer. All of us would like to think that we are "better" than Jeffrey Dahmer and that we're definitely not as bad as he was. Or we're not as "bad" as he was.

Jeffrey Dahmer and Mother Teresa

But when the smoke clears, I think there is a truth here we must consider. Too many religious people are like the Pharisee who prayed, "God, I thank you that I am not like

other men—robbers, evildoers, adulterers—
or even like this tax collector." He might as
well have said, "I thank God I'm not like Jeffrey Dahmer." Well, it's true. He wasn't like
Jeffrey Dahmer. And he didn't experience
God's grace either. He went home still in his
sins, while the hated tax collector who in
humility prayed, "God, be merciful to me, a
sinner," ended up justified by God (see Luke
18:9–14 for the story Jesus told).

As long as you think you are better than
other people, you are not ready to be saved
from your sin because you have not yet considered how great your sin really is. Jesus did
not come to save "semi" sinners or "partial"
sinners or "not-so-bad" sinners. As long as you
feel the need to put some kind of qualifying
adjective before the word "sinner," you aren't
ready to come to Jesus. You won't see your
need for the grace of God.

To put the matter this way is not to deny
the real moral differences among people. Is
there no difference between Jeffrey Dahmer
and Mother Teresa? Of course there is. One
was a sadistic killer, the other an instrument of
God's mercy to multitudes of hurting people.
But our perspective is all-important. Let's suppose that we throw Jeffrey Dahmer into the

deepest pit on earth. Then let's travel to the top of the Sears Tower in downtown Chicago. There we will look over the railing and jeer at Jeffrey Dahmer and congratulate ourselves for being so far above him. Now consider what God sees. From heaven He looks down as if the earth is a trillion miles away. What happens to the distance between us and Jeffrey Dahmer? It vanishes from God's point of view. That's why Romans 3:22 says, "There is no difference." And that's why the next verse says, "For all have sinned and fall short of the glory of God." We're all in the same boat—like it or not.

Wanted:
A Righteous Man

For sixteen years I served as pastor of a church in Oak Park, Illinois. During a sermon one Sunday, I said that there were no righteous people in Oak Park. None at all. The next Sunday, a woman shook my hand and said she wanted to ask me a question. I could tell that she was deeply concerned about something. "Last week you said there was no one righteous in all of Oak Park." That's true. I did indeed say that, and I also said there were no righteous people in any of the surrounding cities and towns. Apart from God's grace, there is no righteousness to be found anywhere. With a face marked with intense concern, she asked, "But Pastor Ray, if you aren't a righteous man, where can we find one?"

Her question was honest and sincere. I didn't say what I could have said: "If you only knew me like my family knows me, you wouldn't ask that question." Instead, I told her to listen to my sermon and she would find the answer. I recounted the story to the congregation and said I would show them the only righteous person in Oak Park—or anywhere else for that matter. Pointing to the cross on the wall behind the pulpit, I declared that Jesus is the only righteous man who ever lived.

And compared to Him, I am Jeffrey Dahmer.

Jesus Christ was pure, holy, and perfect in every way. He never sinned, not even one time. Though He was severely tempted, He never gave in. All the rest of us fall so far short that we cannot begin to be compared to Him. He is the only righteous man ever to walk this earth.

And we crucified Him. His reward for doing God's will was death on a bloody Roman cross. Here is the wonder of grace at work.

From the murder of a perfect man came God's plan to rescue the human race.

This, I think, is what Philip Yancey meant when he called grace "scandalous" and "shocking." Indeed it is. To the human heart no doctrine is more repugnant than the doctrine of grace because it forces us to admit that we are truly helpless because of our sin.

Grace Needed

One of our major objections at this point involves the fact that we're not as bad as we could be. We could be worse. After all, we haven't broken all of the Ten Commandments. That's certainly true for most of us, at least in the literal, outward sense. But the Bible says that to break any part of God's Law is the same as breaking all of it. James 2:10 says, "Whoever keeps the whole law and yet stumbles at just one point is guilty of breaking all of it." In that sense, the Ten Commandments are like a ten-link chain that stretches from earth to heaven. If you break one of those links, it doesn't matter how well you keep the other nine. To break one is the same as breaking them all.

This was driven home to me when our children were young and I was watching our two younger sons while my wife went shopping with our oldest son. She hadn't been gone long when I heard a loud crash from the backyard. Before I could even get out of my chair, my youngest son ran inside and said, "Mark broke the glass in the screen door." Then before I went outside to check it, Mark came running up and said, "Don't worry, Dad. I only broke part of it." "Which part was that?" "The part down by the corner."

When I went outside to check, there was a hole about the size of my fist in the lower right-hand corner of the glass. What had happened? Well, the boys had gotten into my golf clubs and were practicing their swings. Evidently Mark's aim was not much better than mine, since he wound up and sent the ball right through the screen door. But, he assured me again, it was okay since he had broken only part of it. I patiently explained to him that it didn't work that way. If you broke any part of the glass, it was as if you had broken it all, since the whole thing had to be replaced.

It's the same way with God's law. There's no such thing as being a "moderate" sinner. That's like being a "little bit" pregnant. You're either a sinner or you're not. If you break any part of God's law, it's as if you've broken the whole thing. You can't repair the situation by trying to make up for your sin in other areas. God won't accept that solution. It doesn't matter how good you think you are; you still stand in need of God's grace.

Grace Given

The Bible puts it this way: "But because of his great *love* for us, God, who is rich in *mercy*, made us alive with Christ even when we were dead in transgressions—it is by *grace* you have been saved" (Ephesians 2:4–5). Check out those italicized words: "love, mercy, grace." Grace means that while we were completely and totally and absolutely dead in our sins, God decided to do something to rescue us. Love is God reaching out to His creatures in kindness. Mercy is God withholding punishment that we rightly deserve. Think of it this way. Imagine a vast reservoir of God's love. As it begins to flow toward us, it becomes a river of mercy. As it cascades down upon us, the mercy becomes a torrent of grace. Here's a good way to remember the difference between mercy and grace:

⇨Mercy is God not giving us what we do deserve—judgment.

⇨Grace is God giving us what we don't deserve—salvation.

The picture of a mighty river of grace washing over us is especially helpful, since grace always comes down from God to man. Grace never goes up; it always comes down. Grace by definition means that God gives us what we don't deserve and could never earn.

Grace Received

How is grace communicated to the human heart? Ephesians 2:8–9 gives us the answer: "For it is by grace you have been saved, through faith—and this not from yourselves, it is the gift of God—not by works, so that no one can boast." Grace comes to us through faith, not by works, not by religion, not by anything we might conceive as "earning" God's favor. Grace saves us through faith. Nothing more, nothing less. Something in us always wants to add to God's free grace. It's humbling to admit that we can do nothing to earn our deliverance from sin. But any time we add anything to grace, we subtract from its meaning.

Grace must be free or else it is not grace at all. Free grace? Of course. What other kind could there be?

Grace is the source, faith is the means, and salvation is the result. Or you might say that grace is the reservoir, faith is the channel, and salvation is the stream that washes my sin away. And all of it is the gift of God, even the faith that lays hold of God's grace. Even our faith is not of us. It, too, is part of God's gift. Our situation is so hopeless that salvation must come from another place. We need help that comes from outside ourselves. We are not saved by what we do but by what Jesus Christ has done for us.

We are saved by grace through faith:

⇨Apart from works
⇨Apart from all human "goodness"

That salvation is freely given and is received by faith alone.

"You and Me, Jesus"

This view of grace is hard for good people to accept because it means we must give up our "goodness" in order to be saved. We must admit that nothing we have done matters in the least when it comes to being forgiven by God. What would heaven be like if you had to earn your way there? It would be like going to one of those $500-per-plate political dinners where people stand around bragging about how much they gave to help their candidate win the election. "I gave $5,000." "So what? I gave $10,000." "Big deal. I gave $50,000." "Move out of the way, pipsqueak. I own this guy. He's got $300,000 of my money." And so it goes.

Heaven would be just like that if you had to earn your way there. "I was a leader at my church." "I made audio recordings for the blind." "I gave a million dollars to world missions." "I helped old ladies cross the street." "I changed dressings for burn victims." As good as those things are, they will not help forgive even one sin. They will not save you or help save you.

Wouldn't it be horrible to spend eternity listening to people brag about what they did to earn their salvation? Heaven would not be heaven if that were the case. Someone would put his arm around Jesus and say, "You and me, Jesus, we did it. You died on the cross and I baked the cookies."

When Jesus died on the cross, He paid the full price for your salvation. It doesn't matter whether you baked the cookies or not. Jesus paid the price all by Himself. Entrance into heaven is limited to those who trust Jesus Christ—and Him alone—for their salvation.

One Thousand Points to Go to Heaven!

The following story is totally imaginary but it makes an important point. The scene: St. Peter is manning the entrance desk by the gates of heaven. Up comes a fine-looking man, all dressed up. When he rings the bell, St. Peter says, "Can I help you?" And the man says, "I would like to have entrance into heaven." And St. Peter says, "Excellent. We're certainly glad to have you. We always want more people in heaven."

Then St. Peter says, "In order to enter heaven you have to earn a thousand points." The man says, "That shouldn't be any problem. I have been a very good man all my life. I've been very involved in civic things. I have always given a lot of money to charitable causes. For twenty-five years I was the chairman of the YMCA." As St. Peter writes it all down, he says, "That's a marvelous record. That's one point."

Taken aback, the man adds, "I was married to my wife for forty-five years. I was always faithful. We had five children—three boys and two girls. I always loved them and spent a lot of time with them and made sure they got a good education. I always took good care of them and they turned out so well. I was a real family man." St. Peter says, "I'm very impressed. We don't get too many people up here like you. That's another point."

Sweating freely by now, the man starts shaking. "You don't understand. I was active in my church. I went every Sunday. I gave money every time they passed the plate. I was a deacon and an elder. I even sang in the choir. I taught Sunday school for twenty years." And St. Peter says, "Your record is certainly admirable. That's another point." Then he adds, "Let me add this up. That's one, two, three points. Only 997 to go."

Trembling, the man falls to his knees. In desperation he cries out, "But for the grace of God nobody could get in here!" St. Peter looks at him and smiles, "Congratulations, you've just received one thousand points."

For Sinners Only

Do you want to go to heaven? You've got to get there by the grace of God or you won't get there at all. Salvation begins when a person understands that he cannot save himself. The door to heaven has a sign over the top that reads "For Sinners Only." If you qualify, you can go to heaven.

In the end, grace means that no one is too bad to be saved. Are there any truly bad people reading this chapter? I have some good news for you. God specializes in saving really bad people. Do you have some things in your background that you would be ashamed to talk about in public? Fear not. God knows all about it, and His grace is greater than your sin.

Grace also means that some people may be too "good" to be saved. That is, they may have such a high opinion of themselves that they think they don't need God's grace. They may admit they are sinners, but they won't admit they are spiritually dead. They may think they're sick because of sin but not truly dead. God's grace cannot help you until you are desperate enough to admit you need it.

The Church of the Nativity in Bethlehem is built over the reputed spot where Mary gave birth to Jesus. To get to the church, you first walk across a broad plaza and then come to a very small entrance. In fact, it's so small that you have to duck down low to get inside. The entrance is deliberately made so low because several centuries ago the local big shots liked to ride their horses right into the sanctuary. The priests felt that was inappropriate, so they lowered the entrance to force the great men to dismount before entering the church. There is a lesson here for all of us. If you want to go to heaven, you've got to get off your high horse and humble yourself before the Lord. Until you do, you'll never be saved.

That brings me to my final point. How do you find God's grace? Just ask for it. That's all. It's really that simple. The more you feel your need for grace, the better candidate you are to receive it. Hold out your empty hands and ask God for His grace. You will not be turned away.

It's never too late. God says, "Though your sins are like scarlet, they shall be as white as snow" (Isaiah 1:18). That kind of grace is not only amazing, it's shocking and truly "out of this world." Only God would have thought of something like this.

Grace is at the heart of the good news that can change your life. And the best part is, it's free. Stay tuned for even more good news.

A TRUTH TO REMEMBER

Grace never goes up; it always comes down. Grace by definition means that God gives us what we don't deserve and could never earn.

Going Deeper

Ephesians 2:1–10 offers one of the clearest explanations of grace in the Bible. The following questions are based on this passage.

According to verses 1–2, what words or phrases describe our true condition before we come to Christ for salvation?

Verses 4–5 mention three words that describe God's action toward us: love, mercy, and grace. Briefly define each word as it relates to God.

If salvation is by grace and not by works (verses 8–9), why do so many people think they have to do good works in order to go to heaven?

How do you react to the teaching that there is nothing at all you can do to save yourself and that salvation is a free gift from God and must be received by faith alone?

4

A MAN
Called Jesus

WHO IS JESUS CHRIST? Before you answer that question, let me set the scene. It's a few minutes past noon in downtown Philadelphia. You're walking with a few friends to a favorite lunch spot when a camera crew stops you for a spontaneous interview. To your surprise, their questions have nothing to do with politics, the economy, or where you stand on capital punishment. The interviewer wants to know what you think about Jesus Christ. Who is He? While you fumble for an answer, the video camera records your discomfort. You weren't prepared for this, much less dressed for it, and now you're being quizzed on theology while your friends watch from five feet away. The seconds pass as various answers flash across your mental screen: "A good man . . . the Son of God . . . a prophet . . . a Galilean rabbi . . . a teacher of God's Law . . . the embodiment of God's love . . . a reincarnated spirit master . . . the ultimate revolutionary . . . the Messiah of Israel . . . Savior . . . a first-century wise man . . . a man just like any other man . . . King of kings . . . a misunderstood teacher . . . Lord of the universe . . . a fool who thought He was God's Son . . . the Son of Man . . . a fabrication of the early church."

Which answer will you give? Before you answer, let me say that you can find people today who will give every one of those possible answers. But it's nothing new. When Jesus asked His disciples, "Who do people say I am?" they replied with four different answers (see Matthew 16:13–16). Even when He walked on this earth, people were confused as to His true identity. Some thought He was a prophet, others that He was a great political leader, and still others that He was John the Baptist come back to life.

One question with many answers. One man with many faces.

It's not enough to believe in Jesus. You must be certain that the Jesus you believe in

is the right Jesus. In a world of spiritual coun-
terfeits, your eternal destiny depends on knowing the Christ of God who is revealed in the
New Testament.

Who is Jesus Christ? Or to borrow a
phrase, "Will the real Jesus please stand up?"
The only way to discover the real Jesus is to go
to the original source—the Bible. If you would
like to know Jesus personally, here are seven
statements that summarize who He really is.

1. *He had a supernatural entrance into the world*

We know from the Old Testament that
many details of His coming were predicted
hundreds of years before His birth. The
prophet Isaiah predicted He would be born of
a virgin (Isaiah 7:14), and another prophet
named Micah identified His birthplace as
Bethlehem (Micah 5:2). Galatians 4:4 tells us
that He came "in the fullness of time," which
means that God so arranged the circumstances
that He was born at precisely the right moment
in precisely the right way. The great creeds of
the church use this sentence to describe His
birth: "Conceived of the Holy Spirit and born
of the Virgin Mary." Although we often speak
of the "virgin birth," the real miracle took place
nine months before Bethlehem when the Holy

Spirit overshadowed Mary and created within her womb the divine-human person of the Lord Jesus Christ. The fact that He was born of a virgin means He had an earthly mother but no earthly father. No one else has ever been born in this manner.

2. *He was God in human flesh*

Christians use the word "Incarnation" to describe this truth. It means that when Christ was conceived in Mary, God the Son took on human flesh. Though He was God, He added humanity without subtracting from His deity. He was not half-God and half-man, but fully God and fully man, two natures united in one person. He was fully human in every respect, yet without sin. John 1:14 tells us that "the Word became flesh and made his dwelling among us." Hebrews 1:3 says that Jesus is "the radiance of God's glory and the exact representation of his being." The first phrase means that Christ is the "shining forth" of God. He is to God what sunlight is to the sun. The second phrase means that Jesus Christ bears within Himself the exact stamp of the divine nature—like a die being stamped into a piece of metal. When He was born, He was called Immanuel, "God with us." Jesus was the Son of God and God the Son. That is why when the apostle Thomas finally saw the resurrected Christ, he fell on his face and cried, "My Lord and my God!" (John 20:28).

3. *He is the standard of absolute righteousness*

When Jesus Christ walked on the earth, He was perfectly righteous. This speaks to two sides of His character. On the negative side, He never sinned in thought, word, or deed. He is the only "Perfect 10" who ever lived. All the rest of us have fallen far short of perfection, but not Jesus. Hebrews 4:15 says that Jesus was "tempted in every way, just as we are—yet was without sin." He did not sin outwardly because He did not sin inwardly. He was without fault and without evil. He never had an evil thought, never said an evil word, never committed even one evil deed. He never cheated, never lied, never procrastinated, never got bitter, never lost His temper, never lusted, never sought an easy way out of a hard situation, never bent the truth to make Himself look good, never cursed, never turned His back on His friends, never broke any laws of God, and never deviated in the slightest degree from the path of His Father's will. Of all the billions of people who have lived on planet Earth, He is the only one about whom it can be truly said that He never sinned in word, in thought or in deed. There is no hint of moral contamination surrounding His name.

On the positive side, this means He perfectly fulfilled God's law. He lived a life of perfect holiness, perfect purity, perfect kindness, perfect truth, and perfect goodness. Just as Adam sinned and all humanity fell with him, even so Christ through His obedience to God won salvation for all those who follow Him. He succeeded where we failed, and He obeyed where we rebelled. By His perfect life, He fulfilled everything that God required of us.

4. *He did things only God can do*

He made amazing claims and then backed them up with amazing deeds. He repeatedly claimed equality with God. "I and the Father are one" (John 10:30). He also said, "Anyone who has seen me has seen the Father" (John 14:9). He spoke with divine authority: "I am the living water"; "I am the light of the world"; "I am the way, the truth, and the life." He even claimed the ability to raise Himself from the dead (John 5:25) and proved it by raising Lazarus from the dead (John 11:38–43).

People who are only vaguely familiar with Jesus tend to underestimate this part of His teaching. They like to label Him as a great moral teacher while discounting His (to them) more outlandish claims. But as British professor and Christian author C. S. Lewis remarked, a person who talked like Jesus talked, if He wasn't who He said He was, wouldn't be a good teacher. He would be a liar, or a lunatic, or the Devil of hell, or something worse. You can't have Jesus without dealing with His claims of deity.

He backed up those claims by repeatedly demonstrating power over the forces of nature, sickness, and death. He even claimed the power to forgive sins (Matthew 9:2). This is what initially got Him in trouble with the Jewish leaders. They rightly saw Jesus as claiming to be God, but they drew the wrong conclusion. He claimed to forgive sins because He was indeed God in human flesh.

5. *He died as a sacrifice for our sins*

The story of His earthly life ends this way. Though innocent of all wrongdoing, He was crucified as a common criminal. Pontius Pilate, the Roman governor, three times declared, "I find him not guilty" (John 18:38; 19:4, 6 NLT).

The Bible says He died as the just for the unjust, the innocent for the guilty, the good for the bad. He died as our substitute, standing in our place, taking our punishment, bearing our sins in His own body. "Christ died for sins once for all, the righteous for the unrighteous, to bring you to God" (1 Peter 3:18). With His own blood He paid the full price for our disobedience. In so doing He completely satisfied God's righteous demands and enabled God to be merciful to sinners who come to Him in Jesus' name. Through His death we are set free from the penalty of sin forever.

6. *He proved His claims by rising from the dead*

In many discussions with His disciples, Jesus openly predicted His death and His resurrection. In John 10:17 He declared, "I lay down my life—only to take it up again." Nothing that happened came as a surprise to Him. He knew it all and saw it all long in advance. Late on the evening of Good Friday, His followers tenderly took His dead body from the cross. Wrapping Him in grave cloths, they laid His corpse in a borrowed tomb not far from Skull Hill, the place where He died. On Saturday, the Romans, the Jews, and the disciples agreed on only one thing: Jesus was truly dead. Because of fears that someone might disturb the grave and remove His body, an elite squad of Roman soldiers stood guard at His tomb, which was sealed and covered with an enormous stone.

That was Saturday. Early on Sunday morning, when Mary and the other women came to the tomb, they planned to anoint His dead body. But instead they found the soldiers unconscious on the ground, the seal broken, the stone rolled away, and angels guarding the entrance. The angels announced that Jesus had risen from the dead. "Why do you look for the living among the dead? He is not here; he has risen!" (Luke 24:5–6). The women were confused and frightened and reported to the other disciples that the tomb was empty. Later that day, and many times over the next forty days, Jesus appeared in bodily form to His disciples as well as to over five hundred other people. Then He ascended into heaven where He now sits at the Father's right hand.

After two thousand years, skeptics have never provided a sufficient answer to this question: What happened to the body of Jesus? No one ever found His dead body because by Easter Sunday it wasn't dead anymore. There is no other reasonable answer than this: Jesus Christ actually, literally, and physically rose from the dead. And from that day to this, the Christian church has made the resurrection the cornerstone of the gospel message.

The resurrection of Jesus is vitally important because it proves that He really is the Son of God and that everything He said is true. No one else has ever come back from the dead never to die again. This means that in the most profound sense Jesus Christ is alive today. And that's why you can know Him personally. Because He is alive, He gives eternal life to those who trust in Him. And because He conquered death, those who trust in Him need not fear death, for they have assurance that they will go to heaven to be with the Lord Jesus when they die. When He returns to the earth, their bodies will be raised from the dead. All this is guaranteed to the believer because Christ rose from the dead.

7. *He will one day return to the earth*

With this final fact, we move from the distant past to the not-so-distant future. There is yet one more event in the "career" of Jesus Christ. One day He will return to the earth. He promised to return—"I will come again"

(John 14:3 KJV)—and He will keep that promise. He will come just as He left—visibly and bodily. "This same Jesus, who has been taken from you into heaven, will come back in the same way you have seen him go into heaven" (Acts 1:11). His coming is not merely spiritual but actual and literal. This is truly an astounding thought. The same Jesus who was born in Bethlehem, walked on this earth, died on the cross, rose from the dead, and ascended into heaven is coming again. The actual, historical figure who lived two thousand years ago on the other side of the world is returning to the earth one more time. Although no one knows the day or the hour, the fact of His return is certain.

The Christ We Need

Let's now wrap up this chapter with a simple thought. Only the Christ revealed in the pages of Holy Scripture can save us. But the Jesus of the Bible is not the only "Jesus" in the marketplace of ideas. To be almost right about Jesus is to be totally wrong. Why? Because we are not saved by good opinions about Jesus. We are not saved because we have a good feeling about Jesus. We are not saved because we like His moral teaching. We are saved by trusting in all that Jesus accomplished for us in His obedient life, His sacrificial death, and His bodily resurrection from the dead.

A Cop's Cop

I've never forgotten a police officer I met while living in California. He had been a cop's cop. He was tough with a capital T. He had seen the underside of life, and it had left him jaded and skeptical. Before he was a cop, he had served in Vietnam and had seen some horrible things. I think that's what made him live "on the edge."

He lived right across the street from the church where I served as pastor, and his children occasionally came to Sunday school— and he and his wife would sometimes show up for a worship service. Over the months we struck up a friendship—mostly because he told the most incredible stories I had ever heard in my life. He was what you would call a "seeker." For a long time, he plied me with one question after another about the Bible and Jesus Christ, not hostile or negative but sincerely looking for the truth. He wanted to know if he could trust the Bible and if Jesus really was who He claimed to be.

One day we went to eat at a little hole-in-the-wall restaurant where they made the best tacos in town. "Let me tell you what happened to me," he said. And he proceeded to tell me that after carefully investigating all the facts, he had recently trusted Jesus Christ as Lord and Savior. "As I was reading the Bible, suddenly it hit me, 'This stuff is true!'" he declared. I will never forget his description of what happened to him: "It felt like a thousand pounds had been lifted off my shoulders."

That's what it means to encounter the real Christ of the Bible. The weight of sin is lifted off your shoulders. The guilt is gone because your sins have been forgiven.

If Jesus is who He said He is, there is no truth more worthy of your time, no person more important to know. The Christian church is made up of men and women who confess one revolutionary truth—that Jesus of Nazareth is the Son of the living God.

And until you believe that, and confess that, you cannot be called a Christian. It matters not that you may have positive feelings about Jesus Christ or that you think He was a very good man. You are not a Christian until you confess that Jesus is the Savior sent from heaven who is the Son of the Living God.

We end this chapter where we started—

with a most important question: Who is Jesus Christ? A good man? A great teacher? One of the finest fellows who ever walked the face of this earth? Or is He the Son of the Living God who came to be our Savior?

Who is Jesus Christ? Spend a moment thinking how you would respond. Your answer determines your eternal destiny.

A TRUTH TO REMEMBER

If Jesus is who He said He is, there is no truth more worthy of your time, no person more important to know.

Going Deeper

In what way is Jesus different from every other religious leader in history? What evidence backs up the astounding claims He made for Himself?

What is the chief stumbling block that keeps people from believing that Jesus was God in human flesh? If you personally don't believe or are not sure that Jesus was and is truly God, how do you account for what He said and did?

What are the implications for all of humanity if Jesus truly is God?

If Jesus is who He said He is, what are the implications of rejecting that truth (John 8:24)?

What claims did Jesus make about Himself?

> I am the _____ of life (John 6:48).
>
> I am the _____ of the world (John 8:12).
>
> I am from _____ (John 8:23).
>
> I am the good_____ (John 10:11).
>
> I am the _____ and the _____ (John 11:25).
>
> I am the _____, the _____, and the _____ (John 14:6).

5

IT IS
Finished

FRIDAY MORNING in Jerusalem. Another hot April day. Death is in the air. Word has spread to every corner of the city. The Romans plan to crucify somebody today.

A crowd gathers on the north end of town. Just outside the Damascus Gate is a place called Skull Hill. The Romans like it because the hill is beside a main road. That way lots of people can watch the crucifixions carried out there. On this day more people than usual have gathered. They come out of the morbid human fascination with the bizarre. The very horror of crucifixion draws people to Skull Hill.

This day seems like any other, but it is not.

A man named Jesus is being crucified. The word spreads like wildfire. His reputation has preceded Him. No one is neutral. Some believe, many doubt, and a few hate Him.

Three Hours of Darkness

The crucifixion begins at nine o'clock sharp. The Romans are punctual about things like that. At first the crowd is rowdy, loud, raucous, boisterous, as if this were some kind of athletic event. They cheer, they laugh, they shout, they place wagers on how long the men being crucified will last. It appears that the man in the middle will not last long. He has already been severely beaten. In fact, it looks like four or five soldiers have taken turns working Him over. His skin hangs from his back in tatters, His face is bruised and swollen, His eyes nearly shut. Blood trickles from a dozen open wounds. He is an awful sight to behold.

There are voices from all three crosses, a kind of hoarse conversation shouted above the din. Sentence fragments float through the air. Something that sounds like "Father, forgive them," something else about "If you are the Son of God," then a promise of paradise. Finally Jesus spots His mother and speaks to her.

Then it happens. At noon "darkness falls upon all the land." It happens so suddenly that it startles everyone. One moment the sun is right overhead; the next moment it has disappeared. This is not an eclipse, nor is it a dark cloud cover. It is darkness itself, thick, inky-black darkness that falls like a shroud over the land. It is darkness without any hint of light to come. It is chilling blackness that curdles the blood and freezes the skin.

No one moves. No one speaks. For once, even the profane soldiers stop their swearing. Not a sound breaks the dark silence over Skull Hill. Something eerie is going on. It is as if some evil force has taken over the earth and is somehow breathing out the darkness. You can almost reach out and feel the evil all around. From somewhere deep in the earth there is a sound like some dark subterranean chuckle. It is the laughter of hell.

The darkness lasts for three long hours: 12:30—still dark. 1:15—still dark. 2:05—still dark. 2:55—still dark.

3:00 p.m. And just as suddenly as the darkness descended, it disappears. Voices now, and shouting. Rubbing the eyes to adjust once again to the bright sunlight. Panic on many faces, confusion on others. A man leans over to his friend and cries out, "What in God's name is going on here?"

Mortally Wounded

All eyes focus on the center cross. It is clear the end is near. Jesus is at the point of death. Whatever happened in those three hours of darkness has brought Him to death's door. His strength is nearly gone, the struggle almost over. His chest heaves with every tortured breath; His moans now are only whispers. Instinctively the crowd pushes closely to watch His last moments.

One glance at the middle cross makes clear that this man Jesus will not last much longer. He looks dead already. The soldiers know from years of experience that He won't make it to sundown.

Then it happens. He shouts something: "My God, My God, why have you forsaken me?" Someone in the crowd shouts back to Him. Moments pass, death draws near, then a hoarse whisper. "I thirst." The soldiers put some sour vinegar on a sponge, which they lift to His lips on a stalk of hyssop. He moistens His lips and takes a deep breath. If you listen, you can hear the death rattle in His throat. He has less than a minute to live.

Then He speaks again. It is a quick shout. Just one word. If you aren't paying attention, you miss it in all the confusion. He breathes out another sentence. Then He is dead.

What is that shout? "It is finished" (John 19:30).

In the original language of the New Testament, that phrase comes from a word that means "to bring to an end, to complete, to accomplish." It's a crucial word because it signifies the successful end to a particular course of action. It's the word you would use when you reach the peak of Mt. Everest. It's the word you would use when you turn in the final copy of your term paper. It's the word you would use when you make the final payment on your new car. It's the word you would use when you cross the finish line of your first 10K run. The word means more than just "I survived." It means "I did exactly what I set out to do."

"It is finished" was the Savior's final cry of victory. When He died, He left no unfinished business behind. When He said, "It is finished," He was speaking the truth.

Paid in Full

In the Greek language, the phrase "It is finished" also means "Paid in full." Once a thing is paid for, you never have to pay for it again. That point came home to me several years ago when we visited some friends in western Colorado. When I called the husband and said we would be passing through their area, he said they would be glad to put us up. I assumed that we would be camping on sofas for the night—which was fine with us—but when I called him from southern Utah to let him know we would arrive in three or four hours, he said that he had a room for us at the local hotel—the Back Narrows Inn. I thought he was kidding. But he was serious. "Our house isn't big enough"—they had moved since we came through a few years before—"so we'll put you up in the hotel." When I protested, he said, "Don't worry about it. I've worked it out with the owner, and I've already taken care of the bill." That was that. We were staying at the hotel and he was paying. And nothing I could say would make the slightest difference.

We got to the Back Narrows Inn at about 10:00 p.m. and found it to be a small, turn-of-the-century building that had been converted into a fifteen- or twenty-room hotel. When we arrived, the owner greeted us, handed us our keys, and said, "Your friend has taken care of everything." Indeed he had. We didn't even have to formally check in. No credit cards, no filling out forms, no "How will you be paying for this, sir?" It wasn't necessary because my friend had personally paid the price in full. All that was left to us was to enjoy our rooms, provided free of charge to us by virtue of a friend's hospitality. I couldn't pay twice because my friend had already paid once. To attempt to pay on my own would be to insult my friend and to doubt that he had actually paid anything at all.

Why Jesus Had to Die

Several years ago a talk-show host listed the various reasons why he had become disillusioned with Christianity. Among them was this: "How could an all-knowing, all-loving God allow His Son to be murdered on a cross to redeem my sins?" That's an excellent question because it goes to the very heart of the gospel.

Many people hear the gospel and wonder why Jesus had to die. How could an all-knowing, all-loving God allow His Son to be murdered on a cross to redeem guilty sinners? In searching for the answer, it helps me to think of another question: Since God is both all-powerful and infinitely gracious, why didn't

He simply offer forgiveness to anyone who says "I'm sorry"? Many people secretly think that's what God should have done. Then they wouldn't have to deal with the "embarrassment" of God putting His own Son to death.

The solution to the dilemma goes like this. From a human point of view, God had a problem. Because God is holy, He cannot allow sin to go unpunished. His justice demands that every sin be punished—no matter how small it may seem to us. If He were to forgive sin without proper punishment, He would cease to be holy and just. God would no longer be God because He would have denied His own character. That could not happen. All offenses against God must be punished. That's why sinners can't simply say "I'm sorry," and instantly be forgiven. Someone has to pay the price.

We often see this principle at work in the family. Through carelessness, or perhaps through deliberate disobedience, a five-year-old boy breaks an expensive lamp in the living room. Realizing what he has done, he apologizes to his father and mother, and promises never to do it again. The parents forgive their son, but the lamp is still broken. Someone has to pay for the lamp.

We follow this same principle in our criminal justice system. Suppose a man is found guilty of stealing $700,000 from his employer. Just before sentencing, he stands before the judge, confesses his crime, begs for mercy, and promises never to steal money again. How would you react if the judge accepted his apology and released him with no punishment? Suppose the man had been convicted of rape and then was set free with no punishment simply because he apologized? Or what if he apologized for murdering a father and mother in front of their children—and the judge set him free? Suppose a terrorist infiltrates a military installation and opens fire, killing dozens of soldiers in the process. And suppose at his trial he admits his crime and apologizes. What would we do if the judge released him on a promise never to do it again? We would put that judge in jail and throw away the key.

Even in this life a price must be paid for breaking the law. The same is true in the spiritual realm. "The wages of sin is death" (Romans 6:23). When sin is not punished, it doesn't seem very sinful. God's "problem" was to devise a plan of salvation whereby He would remain holy and just and still provide a way of forgiveness for guilty sinners. Somewhere, somehow, there had to be a place where grace and wrath could meet. That place is the cross of Christ.

Back to that talk-show host for a moment. He asked a second question that deserves an answer: "If God the Father is so 'all-loving,' why didn't He come down and go to Calvary?" The answer is, He did! God came down to this earth in the person of His Son, the Lord Jesus Christ, and died for our sins.

God is a God of love and therefore wants to forgive sinners. But He is also a God of holiness who must not and cannot overlook sin. How could God love sinners and yet not overlook their sin? No one would ever have dreamed of His answer. God sent His own Son to die for sinners. "But God shows his great love for us in this way: Christ died for us while we were still sinners" (Romans 5:8 NCV). In that way, the just punishment for sin was fully met in the death of Christ, and sinners who trust in Christ could be freely forgiven. Only God could have done something like that.

Think of it. In the death of this one man, the price for sin has been fully paid for—past, present, and future. As a result, those who believe in Jesus find that their sins are gone forever.

This is truly good news: God's holiness

demands that sin be punished. God's grace provides the sacrifice. What God demands, He supplies. Thus salvation is a work of God from first to last. It is conceived by God, provided by God, and applied by God.

Name Your Sin

So let me ask you a personal question. What sin is keeping you from God right now? Is it anger? Is it lust? Is it a hard heart of unbelief? Is it alcohol abuse? Is it an uncontrollable temper? Is it cheating? Is it gambling? Is it stealing? Is it adultery? Is it abortion? Is it pride? Is it greed?

Let me tell you the best news you've ever heard. It doesn't matter what "your" sin is. It doesn't matter how many sins you've piled up in your life. It doesn't matter how guilty you think you are. It doesn't matter what you've been doing this week. It doesn't matter how bad you've been. It doesn't matter how many skeletons rattle around in your closet.

When you come to Christ, you discover that all of your sins have been stamped by God with this phrase: Paid in full.

Anger . . .   Paid in Full
Uncontrolled ambition . . . Paid in Full

Gossip . . .	Paid in Full
Drunkenness . . .	Paid in Full
Fornication . . .	Paid in Full
Stealing . . .	Paid in Full
Lying . . .	Paid in Full
Disobedience . . .	Paid in Full
Laziness . . .	Paid in Full
Pride . . .	Paid in Full
Murder . . .	Paid in Full
Bribery . . .	Paid in Full

Those are just examples. Fill in the blank with whatever sins plague your life. Through the blood of Jesus Christ, the price for "your" sins has been paid in full.

Two Simple Statements

Let me sum up what this means in two simple statements:

First, since Jesus Christ paid in full, the work of salvation is now complete. That is what Jesus' statement "It is finished" means. The debt was paid, the work was accomplished, the sacrifice was completed. It means that when Jesus died, He died once for all time. The sacrifice was sufficient to pay for the sins of every person who has ever lived—past, present, or future. Hebrews 7:25 says that Jesus "is able to save completely those who come to God through him." The word "completely" has the idea of "entirely" and "forever." It means that the work of salvation has been fully accomplished by Jesus Christ.

And that explains what Christians mean when they talk about the "finished work" of Jesus Christ. That's not just a slogan; it's a profound spiritual truth. What Jesus accomplished in His death was so awesome, so total, so complete that it could never be repeated. Not even by Jesus Himself. His work is "finished." There is nothing more God could do to save the human race. There is no Plan B. Plan A (the death of Christ) was good enough.

Second, since Jesus Christ paid in full, all efforts to add anything to what Christ did on the cross are doomed to failure. Let me put it very simply. If Jesus paid it all, you don't have to pay anything. If you try to pay for your salvation, it means you don't think He paid it all. There is no middle ground between those two propositions. That's why going to church, obeying the Ten Commandments, increasing your education, doing good works, giving money to the poor, being baptized, improving your life, turning over a new leaf, being a nice person, working hard at your marriage, raising model children, and trying to do your best can be such a trap. Those things, good as they are, cannot add anything to the value of what Jesus accomplished in His death on the cross. They will not help you take even one tiny step toward God. In the end it is either all by Jesus or not by Jesus at all.

God is not trying to sell you salvation. He's not offering salvation at half-price. He's not offering salvation on an installment plan. He's not offering you salvation where he pays part of the cost and you pay the rest. God is offering you salvation free of charge. Jesus paid in full so you wouldn't have to pay anything. Jesus left no unfinished business behind. He finished what He came to do. If you will trust Him, you will discover that in finishing His work, He paid in full the price for your sin.

A TRUTH TO REMEMBER

What Jesus accomplished in his death was so awesome, so total, so complete that it could never be repeated, not even by Jesus Himself.

Going Deeper

Read Romans 5:7. How many people would you die for right now, no questions asked? Romans 5:8 says that while we were still _____, Christ died for us.

According to Hebrews 9:22, what is required for the forgiveness of sin?

Even our good deeds are like what in the eyes of God? (Isaiah 64:6)

According to Hebrews 9:22, what is required for the forgiveness of sin?

What does the blood of Jesus Christ do for us? (I John I:7)

6

THE GREAT
Exchange

WHAT'S YOUR CREDIT like with God? If God is the Great Creditor, are you "in the red" or "in the black" as far as He is concerned?

That question came to mind one day as I opened my mail at home. As I sorted the envelopes into two piles, it seemed as if everything we received that day was either a credit card bill or an invitation to apply for more credit cards. Some of the invitations were quite seductive. Low interest rates, the opportunity to get "free" merchandise and special, super-discounts on certain items that I would probably never buy at any price.

Let's take the concept of credit into the spiritual realm. How much credit do you have with God? The Bible offers a surprising answer to that question. We are all born spiritually bankrupt and spend our lives overdrawing on an account that is already far gone "in the red." But because of what Christ accomplished on the cross, God allows bankrupt sinners who have no hope of creditworthiness, to "borrow" whatever they need based on His Son's unlimited credit in heaven. Then God pays the debt once for all! Romans 4 tells us how we can get our lives out of spiritual debt and end up on the plus side of the ledger.

The Heart of the Gospel

In this chapter we have finally arrived at the heart of the good news. We have already seen that when Jesus died, He paid in full for our sins. How does that apply to you and me? The answer is that God justifies wicked people who trust in Him. Romans 4:5 puts it this way: "However, to the man who does not work but trusts God who justifies the wicked, his faith is credited as righteousness" Here we learn that God justifies (declares righteous) wicked people who trust in him. He credits their account in heaven with the righteousness of Jesus Christ. Thus, the guilty are acquitted on the basis of what Jesus Christ did when He died on the cross and rose from the dead.

Why Working Won't Work

We begin with an astounding statement. When God acquits the guilty, He first finds a person who isn't working for his acquittal. Romans 4:5 says that God justifies the person "who does not work." God looks for people who don't want to work for what they get. On the face of it, that's an incredible statement. Most of us have been raised to believe that nothing is truly free in life. You get what you work for. Work hard and you will be rewarded at the end of the day. If you don't work, you won't get ahead. True as that may be in everyday life, it's not true with regard to eternal salvation. In order for God to save you, you've got to stop working for it.

Lots of people (most people, actually) follow this motto—"We get our salvation the old-fashioned way. We earn it." But God's salvation is not a do-it-yourself kit. If you want to go to heaven, the first step is to stop trying to earn your way there. You have to "stop working" and "start trusting" if you want to be saved. Write it in big letters. When it comes to saving your soul, WORKS DON'T WORK!

What God Wants from Us

If God doesn't want our "works," what does He want from us? He wants us to trust Him. That's all. Nothing more, nothing less, nothing else. In the New Testament, the terms "faith," "trust," and "belief" all come from the same general root word meaning "to lean wholly upon," as when you lie down on a bed, resting your whole weight upon it. We are to trust God so completely that we take Him at His Word regarding our salvation. That's why Romans 4:5 says God justifies the person "who does not work but trusts God."

One crucial distinction must be made. To say that we must trust God does not mean that our faith is something we ourselves do. Faith is not a work that "merits" salvation. Faith is the *condition*, not the *ground* of salvation. Faith cannot save us unless our faith is based upon the person and work of the Lord Jesus Christ, who died for our sins.

What is faith? Faith is the open window that lets the sunlight in. Where did the light come from? From the sun, not from the window. The window simply allows it to enter. By faith we open the windows of our heart to let the light of the gospel shine on us. Faith looks to the cross and says, "Jesus Christ died for me." Faith cries out to God, "Be merciful to me, a sinner, for Jesus' sake." And God hears that prayer every time.

"Not Guilty!"

The word "justify" means to declare "righteous." It is a legal term that refers to the final verdict by which a judge declares that an accused person is "not guilty" and is "innocent" of all charges. Applied to the spiritual realm, it means that God declares the believing sinner righteous on the basis of the death and resurrection of Jesus Christ. Since Christ paid the penalty for the sinner, the sinner is now righteous in the eyes of the Lord. Though the sinner is truly guilty, through faith he receives the benefit of Christ's death on his behalf. Jesus paid the penalty, and the sinner goes free. If you are justified, it means that in the record book by your name there are no marks against you. It means the charges are dropped. There is no guilt, no penalty, no condemnation.

Here are four words that describe justification: It is A) **Complete**—covers all we have done. There are no "half-pardons" with God, B) **Divine**—because it comes from God, C) **Irreversible**—because it is divine, and D) **Free**—received by grace through faith.

Romans 4:5 says that God justifies the wicked. This is hard for many people to accept. Many people think God wants good people in heaven, so they spend their lives trying to be good enough to go there when they die. Wrong! No one can ever be good enough to go to heaven. So many of us are mixed up on this point. We think God is saying, "Clean up your act and then I'll save you." Or we think God is saying, "I'll clean up your act and then I'll save you." God never says any such thing. He says something entirely different: "I'll save you while you are still dirty, and then I'll help you clean up your act." Mark it down. God saves the ungodly while they are still ungodly. That's the miracle of justification. And when you come to Christ—still dirty and unclean—not only does He save you, but He begins an inner process of cleansing that changes you from the inside out. But He saves you first; then He cleans you up.

Many people don't come to Christ because they feel they aren't good enough. They feel as if they are lost in sexual sin, lost in addiction to alcohol and drugs, trapped in anger or bitterness, chained forever to a terrible, destructive way of life. But God is not in the business of justifying the good. He is in the business of justifying the bad. He doesn't justify the righteous. He justifies the wicked while they are still wicked. A doctor does not heal the healthy. He heals the sick (Luke 5:31–32).

The verdict is just in from heaven, and the bad news is, you are guilty. The good news is, Christ is entirely righteous. If you will accept those two rulings from the court of heaven, an amazing miracle will take place. Christ will take your guilt and exchange it with His righteousness.

Here is where the glory of the gospel is clearly seen. It provides for us what we could never provide for ourselves. On our own merit, we all stand condemned before the Almighty. Who would dare to say, "I am good enough to go to heaven"? As someone has said, "A clear conscience is the result of a poor memory." The only people who think they are good enough to go to heaven are the people who don't know how bad they really are. Righteousness is what we need but do not have. Therefore, God, knowing that we could never be righteous on our own, has provided a righteousness which comes down to us from heaven above. It's not earned or deserved, but is given to us by God as a free gift.

Do vs. Done

In this we see the simplicity of Christianity when compared with the religions of the world. Religion is spelled with two letters—D-O. Religion is a list of things people think they have to do in order to be accepted by God—go to church, give money, keep the Ten Commandments, be baptized, pray every day, and do good works. The list is endless. It's always Do . . . Do . . . Do. If you want to go to heaven, you're going to do something and keep on doing it until the day you die.

Christianity is spelled with four letters—D-O-N-E. Christianity is not based on what we do but upon what Jesus Christ has already done. If you want to go to heaven, you don't have to do anything; you just have to trust in what Jesus Christ has already done for you.

That's the whole difference—Do versus Done. Either you do it yourself or you believe that Jesus Christ has already done it for you.

A Tale of Three Socks

Perhaps an illustration will help. Let's begin with three socks—one blue, one red, and one white. The blue sock represents your sin, the red sock represents the blood of Christ, and the white sock represents the righteousness of Christ. Take the blue sock and put it over your right hand. That represents your sin. It covers you so completely that you are a sinner through and through. If you attempt to come into God's presence with your sin exposed, you will be judged and sent to hell. Now put the red sock over the blue one so that it covers the blue (sin) completely. That represents the covering of your sin with the blood of Christ. Then put the white sock over the red one, which is how God sees you in Christ. The white covers the red that covers the blue. Once your sins are covered with the blood, God credits you with the righteousness of His Son, the Lord Jesus Christ. That's the miracle of the gospel.

Swapping Grades with Jesus

But that's only part of the story. Let's further suppose that I have obtained a copy of your transcript with your "official" grades. No, not your high school grades. I'm thinking of something more serious than that. Somehow I have gotten a copy of your "permanent record" from the "Principal's Office" in heaven. Unfortunately, the news is not good. Your grade in every course is the same:

Seeking God — F
Doing Good — F
Obeying God — F
Keeping the Law — F
Being Perfect — F

Not a pretty picture. How would you like it if we changed your grades? I've got some good news to share with you. The valedictorian of the class is quite willing to switch grades. His name is Jesus Christ, and He made an A in each class. Here is your final grade from God:

God's Honor Roll — A

The lesson is simple. If God gave you a report card on your life without Jesus Christ, it would be covered with black marks for all the sins you have committed. Indeed, God gives you and the whole human race an F. You flunk every test. But when you come to Jesus, your F is washed away and your sins are gone forever.

What grade would God give you? You get the grade Christ earned because He finished His course at the top of the class. You don't squeak by with God. You make the honor roll.

You go to the head of the class. Why? Because you are so good? No. Left to yourself you would still flunk every course. If you have trusted Jesus Christ, you get an A because you are united with Him.

The same righteousness that once required that you get an F now requires that you get an A. You are not half-justified and half-condemned. You are not partially forgiven and partially punished. You are altogether forgiven. Your record is wiped clean. You are declared righteous in the eyes of God. That's what justification is all about.

The New York Billionaire

Let's put both sides of the truth together with one final illustration. We begin by supposing that somehow you owe the bank a million dollars. You promise that you will pay back your debt at the rate of $10 per week. On a given day you come to the bank, ready to make your $10 payment. When you hand over the $10 bill, the teller checks your account and says, "According to our records, you don't owe any money at all. In fact, someone has paid your debt and deposited a million dollars in your account."

For a moment you say nothing, stunned by

your sudden good fortune. Who could have done such a thing? Who would have the money to pay the million dollars you owe plus put a million dollars extra into your account? The answer comes as a man steps out of the shadows. From articles you've read, you recognize him as a billionaire from New York. "I paid your debt," he says, "and then I decided to give you a little spending money besides." "Sir, you shouldn't have. I'll try to pay you back someday," you reply. To which the answer comes, "Don't worry. I'm a billionaire ten times over. I've got so much money, I don't know how to spend it all. Don't even think about paying it back. It's a gift."

Could such a thing happen? Yes—at least in my dreams. The billionaire from New York truly does have enough money to do that. In fact, he's got enough money to do that for perhaps five thousand different people. But eventually even he would run out of money.

Not so with Jesus Christ. The New York billionaire is a beggar compared to Him. He can forgive all your sins and give you His perfect righteousness. And He can do the same thing for every other person in the world who comes to Him by faith because His righteousness is infinite and His blood never loses its power.

We can see the whole truth in this one verse. "God made him who had no sin to be sin for us, so that in him we might become the righteousness of God" (2 Corinthians 5:21). When Jesus died on the cross, God treated His Son as if He were a sinner. Jesus so identified with sinners that He was numbered among the transgressors (Isaiah 53:12). He not only died between two sinners, He died as they died—a criminal's death on the cross. As a result, when we trust Christ our sin is credited to Christ's account and His righteousness is credited to our account. He takes our debt and we get his credit. This is the Great Exchange:

⇨He was condemned that we might be justified.

⇨He bore our sin that we might be set free.

⇨He died that we might live.

⇨He suffered that we might be redeemed.

⇨He was made sin that we might be made righteous.

God has a simple proposition for you. If you admit you are a sinner, He offers to declare you righteous. All you have to do is lay hold of Jesus. Trust in Him and your sins will be forgiven, your record in heaven will be wiped clean, and you will be declared righteous in the eyes of God.

Have you ever believed what God has said about His Son, the Lord Jesus Christ?

⇨ He is the Savior of the world and the only way to God.
⇨ He came from heaven for you.
⇨ He died on the cross, paying the price for your sins.
⇨ He rose from the dead on the third day.
⇨ He is ready to forgive you.
⇨ He wants to give you His perfect righteousness.

Have you ever said, "Yes, Lord, I believe those things to be true"? When you get to heaven, you will discover that God is as good as His Word. In the end, it is your faith in Jesus Christ—not your works—that God counts as righteousness.

A TRUTH TO REMEMBER

*God is offering you salvation
free of charge. Jesus paid in full so you
wouldn't have to pay anything.*

Going Deeper

1. Finish this sentence: "If God graded my life thus far, I would probably get a(n) _____."

2. Suppose you died tonight and found yourself at the gate of heaven. How would you answer if God said to you, "Why should I let you into my heaven?"

3. What sort of people does God justify? What encouragement do you take from this truth? (Romans 4:5)

4. God has a simple proposition for you. If you admit you are a sinner, He offers to declare you righteous. All you have to do is come to Jesus. Trust in Him and your sins will be forgiven, your

record in heaven will be wiped clean, and you will be declared righteous in the eyes of God.

_____ I believe this is true.

_____ This doesn't make sense to me.

_____ I need to think about this for a while.

7

WHAT IS
Saving Faith?

THE QUESTION POSED by the title of this chapter is not as easily answered as one might assume. It is evident from reading the New Testament that not everyone who "believes" truly possesses saving faith. Jesus Himself warned in Matthew 7:21–23 (NASB) that on the day of judgment many will claim to have worked miracles in His name, but He will say to them, "I never knew you; depart from Me." And James 2:19 informs us that even the demons believe in God—and tremble because of that belief. Yet they are not saved.

On the other hand when a man asked, "What must I do to be saved?" this simple reply was given, "Believe in the Lord Jesus, and you will be saved" (Acts 16:31). That's clear, isn't it? Believe and be saved. A multitude of verses (especially from the gospel of John) could be added that say the same thing. The problem is not with the words but with their meaning.

That raises a key question. If salvation is based on believing in Christ, how do you know when you have truly believed? We all understand that the word "believe" has many different nuances. For instance, if I say, "I believe it's going to rain tomorrow," that's nothing more than a hunch. Or if I say, "I believe George Washington was the first president of the United States," that refers to a settled historical fact. But if I say, "I believe in Jesus with all my heart," I have made a different sort of statement altogether.

Three Elements of Saving Faith

True saving faith involves the intellect, the emotions, and the will. The faith that saves us involves all that we are in coming to Christ. Faith starts with knowledge, moves to conviction, and ends with commitment. Let's briefly take a look at each element.

1. *Knowledge*

Knowledge refers to the factual basis of the Christian faith. It speaks of intellectual understanding of the truth. You must know something in order to be saved. Faith is based on knowledge, and knowledge is based on truth. The gospel contains information that we need to know. You aren't saved by information, but you can't be saved without it.

Suppose you are in a burning building and cannot find your way out. "Where is the exit?" you cry. Through the smoke and haze comes the answer: "Go down the hallway, turn left, go down one flight of stairs. The exit is on the right." Are you saved because you know where the exit is? No, you still have to make the journey yourself. But if you don't know how to get there, or if you have wrong information, you're going to burn to death. You aren't saved by knowing the truth, but you can't be saved without it.

We must be perfectly clear on this point. Christian faith is not blind faith. We are called to believe in something—not just anything. True saving faith rests first and foremost in Jesus Christ. This is most important. We must know who He is, why He came, why He died, why He rose from the dead, and how He can be our Lord and Savior. I am not suggesting that we must pass a theology exam in order to be saved, but we must know something about these truths if our faith is to rest on the right foundation. Faith must be grounded in the facts of divine revelation. Faith rests on facts, not on thin air. Faith in the wrong thing, however sincere, will not save anyone.

Knowledge is essential, but it alone can never save you. Saving faith begins with knowledge, but it never ends there.

2. *Conviction*

Conviction means to know something and then to be persuaded that it is true. The most common word in the Bible for "believe" means "to have confidence in, to regard as completely reliable." That Hebrew word comes over into English as "Amen," which literally means "Yes, it is true." Saving faith involves saying "Amen" to the facts of the gospel.

A man may go to a doctor who tells him he has cancer. "But there is good news," says the doctor. "We have just discovered a chemotherapy that can cure your cancer. Do you believe it?" "Yes," he answers. Is he cured? No, not until he rolls up his sleeve and lets them stick in the needle and pump the life-saving medicine into his veins.

Conviction is essential because you must be personally convinced of the truth, but that alone cannot save you. There is one final element in true saving faith.

3. *Commitment*

Commitment speaks to the active part of faith. We might use the word "trust" in the sense of "relying fully upon," such as resting with your full weight on a bed, confident that it can hold you up. True faith always reaches out to rest upon some object. If we go to a doctor, we must rest our faith in him. If we go to a lawyer, we must put our case in his hands. This is what is meant by phrases such as "believe in your heart" or "believe with your heart." It means to "embrace" or to "accept" or to "receive" or to "welcome" someone or something.

True saving faith always ends in personal commitment. Sales people understand this principle. After the presentation is made, at some point customers have to sign on the dotted line. If they say, "I know that's a good product," you haven't made a sale. If they say, "I believe I need that," they are closer but you still haven't made a sale. But when they say,

"Where do I sign?" you've just closed the deal.

We can find all three elements of faith in one verse: "I *know* whom I have believed, and am *convinced* that he is able to guard what I have *entrusted* to him for that day" (2 Timothy 1:12). I know . . . and am convinced . . . what I have entrusted. It's all right there. Knowledge, conviction, commitment.

The Great Blondin

In the nineteenth century the greatest tightrope walker in the world was a man named Charles Blondin. On June 30, 1859, he became the first man in history to walk on a tightrope across Niagara Falls. Over twenty-five thousand people gathered to watch him walk 1,100 feet suspended on a tiny rope 160 feet above the raging waters. He worked without a net or safety harness of any kind. The slightest slip would prove fatal. When he safely reached the Canadian side, the crowd burst into a mighty roar.

In the days that followed, he would walk across the Falls many times. Once he walked across on stilts; another time he took a chair and a stove with him and sat down midway across, cooked an omelet, and ate it. Once he carried his manager across riding piggyback.

And once he pushed a wheelbarrow across loaded with 350 pounds of cement. On one occasion he asked the cheering spectators if they thought he could push a man across sitting in a wheelbarrow. A mighty roar of approval rose from the crowd. Spying a man cheering loudly, he asked, "Sir, do you think I could safely carry you across in this wheelbarrow?" "Yes, of course." "Get in," the Great Blondin replied with a smile. The man refused.

That makes it clear, doesn't it? It's one thing to believe a man can walk across by himself. It's another thing to believe he could safely carry you across. But it's something else entirely to get into the wheelbarrow yourself. That's the difference between knowledge, conviction, and commitment.

"That's Amazing!"

If you know what it means to believe a doctor when he says, "You need surgery," you know what it means to have faith. If you know what it means to step into an airplane entrusting your safety to the captain in the cockpit, you know what it means to have faith. If you know what it means to ask a lawyer to plead your case in court, you know what it means to have faith. Faith is total reliance upon another person to do that which you could never do for yourself.

How much faith does it take to go to heaven? It depends. The answer is not much but all you've got. If you are willing to trust Jesus Christ with as much faith as you happen to have, you can be saved. But if you're holding anything back, thinking that maybe you need to do something to help save yourself, forget it!

While serving as a guest host on a national call-in radio program, I took a call from a young girl named Angela, who asked how you can know you are saved. I quoted 1 John 5:13, which says that you can know that you have eternal life through believing in Christ. I told Angela that salvation depends on trusting Jesus Christ. It's more than just believing facts about Jesus. To trust in Christ means to rely completely upon Him. You trust the airline pilot to get you back down on the ground safely. You trust your doctor when you take the medicine he prescribes. You trust your lawyer when you let him represent you in court. God says that when you trust Jesus Christ in that same way you are saved from your sins. All you have to do is trust Christ completely, and you can be saved. When I asked Angela what she thought about that, she blurted out, "Wow! That's amazing." Yes it is. It's the most amazing truth I know.

What about Repentance?

At this point someone may ask where repentance fits into the gospel message. After all, the very first word Jesus spoke in His public ministry was the word "repent" (Matthew 4:17). The word "repentance" literally means "to change the mind." It has to do with the way you think about something. You've been thinking one way, but now you think differently. That's repentance—the changing of the mind.

Let's suppose a man wants to learn how to parachute. So he goes to a skydiving school and they show him how to rig up his gear, how to pull the rip cord, and how to land safely. Finally the day comes when they take him up in an airplane. He's scared to death, but he's too afraid to back out. The moment comes when he is to jump. He goes to the door of the airplane and sees the ground seven thousand feet below. His legs grow weak, he's getting sick, and somebody behind him is trying to push him out of the airplane. At the last second he says, "No. I'm not going to do it."

"Go ahead, you can do it," his instructor shouts. "I've changed my mind," he replies. "I'm not going to jump." And he doesn't. That man has repented. He's changed his mind in a decisive way.

That story illustrates how repentance works. Repentance is a change in the way you think that leads to a change in the way you live. When you really change your mind about something, it's going to change the way you think about it, talk about it, feel about it, and ultimately what you do about it.

True repentance and saving faith go together. They are like two sides of the same coin. According to Mark 1:15, we should "repent and believe the good news!" To repent means to change your mind about whatever is keeping you from coming to Christ. To trust Christ means to wholeheartedly reach out to Him by faith so that He becomes your Savior and Lord.

The Power of Feeble Faith

One day a woman with a serious bleeding problem came to Jesus as He passed along a narrow, crowded street. She reached out, touched the corner of His cloak, and was instantly healed. After twelve years of misery, just one touch and her disease was gone forever. This story is helpful because the woman never said anything to Jesus. No doubt she was both afraid and ashamed to address Him openly. Even after her miraculous healing, she didn't say a word. She simply found Him in the crowd, touched His cloak, was wonderfully healed, and then turned to go. Only at that point did Jesus address her. "Your faith has made you well; go in peace" (Luke 8:48 NASB).

In this poor woman, we see the amazing power of feeble faith. She knew who Jesus was (that's knowledge), she believed He could help her (that's conviction), and she reached out and touched Him in the crowd (that's commitment). She didn't have a huge amount of faith. But she had a tiny grain of faith, and through it, God moved the mountain of her illness.

How simple it is to come to Christ. Only a touch and this woman was healed. Not by her promises to do better, not by an offer to do something for Jesus if He would do something for her. No deals here. She reached out a trembling hand and, in an instant, she was healed. It wasn't even a long process. It happened so fast that it could only be called a miracle.

That's what feeble faith can do. Coming to Christ is not difficult. The hardest part is reaching out with the hand of faith. If you want to touch Jesus, all you have to do is reach out to Him.

That's the power of feeble faith when it is directed toward the right object. You don't have to have strong faith. You can have weak faith as long as it is resting upon a strong object. And who could be stronger than Jesus Christ Himself?

"But my faith is not strong," you say. God never asks if our faith is strong, He only requires that it rest on the Lord Jesus Christ. Even a trembling hand can receive a golden cup. When I receive a gift with my hand, I do not look at my hand and wonder what sort of hand I have. I look to the gift and don't worry about my hand. Don't worry about how strong your faith is. If you have faith enough to want to come to Christ, that's all you need.

Do you ever feel as if your problems keep you from coming to God? Do you ever feel so dirty and unclean that you think Jesus would not have anything to do with you? Do not despair. Jesus is not offended by your problems. He's seen it all before. He will not turn you away.

Christ Standing at the Door

In the last book of the Bible we find the image of Christ standing at the door and knocking. The picture comes from Revelation 3:20, where Christ offers to enter a lukewarm, lethargic church and have fellowship with those who will let Him in. It is a wonderful picture of how Christ comes to each of us. And in this picture we see the three elements of faith made clear.

I hear the knock—That's knowledge
I go to the door—That's conviction
I open the door—That's commitment

Only then does Christ come and make Himself at home in my heart. Years ago I learned a children's chorus that goes like this: "One door and only one, and yet its sides are two. Inside and outside, on which side are you?"

This is a crucial question for all of us to consider. On which side of your heart's door is Jesus Christ? Is He on the inside, or is He on the outside, still knocking, waiting for you to open the door? If you hear Christ knocking, do not delay. Go to the door and let Him in. This is true saving faith.

A TRUTH TO REMEMBER

Saving faith understands the gospel, believes the gospel, and then commits to the gospel as the only hope of salvation. Saving faith reaches out and trusts Christ as Lord and Savior.

Going Deeper

List some religious activities that people may use as a substitute for true saving faith.

According to Hebrews 11:6, what is the one thing necessary in order for us to please God?

Read John 20:26–29. When Thomas finally met Jesus after the resurrection, how did he express his total commitment to Christ?

Let's personalize John 3:16 (ESV). Insert your name in the blanks in this verse. "For God so loved _____, that he gave his only Son, that whoever (_____) believes in him should not perish but have eternal life."

Describe the level of your faith in Jesus Christ at this moment. Is it mostly knowledge without much conviction? Is it conviction without commitment? Or it is knowledge plus conviction plus commitment? If you aren't sure, just say, "I'm not sure" or "I'm still thinking about it."

8

COMING TO
Christ

IF YOU'VE READ THIS FAR, you probably know what comes next. It's time to talk about opening the door and welcoming Christ into your life as Savior and Lord. Before we do that, however, I'd like to share an unusual story of how one man came to Christ. It all started when my friend Bob Johnsen introduced me to his brother Jim. When I met him, Jim was desperately sick with cancer that had returned after some years of remission. Jim could not stand because the pain was so great. We shook hands and he asked me in a desperate voice if I would pray for him. He sounded like a man in need of a Savior but who didn't know where to look. For a month or two I shook his hand each time I saw him in church and tried to encourage him as best I could.

One day Bob called and said that Jim had been taken to the hospital and wanted to see me. When I entered the room, he said, "Pastor, I've got a lot of things I want to tell you." And he slowly unfolded his life story. He told me that as a child he had been raised in a Christian family yet for many years had been away from the Lord. He had spent a long time in the military and was very proud of his service, but during those years he had drifted away from God. "I'm a dead man," he said. "The doctors won't say it, but I know the truth. The cancer is in the spine. I doubt I'll ever get out of the hospital."

He spoke of his years of wandering like the "forty days and forty nights" when the rain came down before the great flood of Noah's day. Something had clearly happened in his life recently, but I didn't know what. Then he told me that one day he heard the familiar children's song: "Jesus Loves Me" and began to sing along. In his own words, as he sang, "it happened." What happened? He trusted Jesus Christ while singing "Jesus loves me," and had a definite conversion experience. It was real, it was clear, it was a powerful change in his life.

As he told me the story, at one point he grabbed my lapel and said, "Pastor Ray, you've got to tell the young. Tell them that Christ is the only answer. The young people need to know this so they won't waste as many years as I did." He then asked me to share his story with everyone I could. "I want to help as many people as I can while I'm still alive."

Then he said something I didn't expect. "I know I'm going to heaven, but there's only one problem. I don't have a certificate." I had no idea what he meant. Evidently some of his friends had said that he needed a certificate to be sure he was going to heaven—perhaps some sort of church membership or baptismal certificate. Whatever the meaning, this troubled him greatly because he had nothing to show to others. Four times he said with great emotion, "But I don't have a certificate." I could tell the matter troubled him greatly.

After I got back to the church, I decided that if Jim needed a certificate, we could give him one. So I wrote down some things and gave it to my assistant. She designed a nice certificate that we printed on a paper with a nice border. After it was signed, we put it in a frame. It said something like this:

Upon the testimony of God's Word
and upon his profession
of faith in Jesus Christ

Jim Johnsen

is a born-again Christian
who has trusted in Jesus Christ
as his Lord and Savior.
"He who has the Son has life;
he who does not have the Son of God
does not have life."
1 John 5:12

"Jesus loves me, this I know,
for the Bible tells me so."

When I gave him the certificate, he wept for forty-five minutes. Later his family placed the certificate on the wall where he could see it. During his last days, he showed the certificate to everyone who visited him. After the funeral, we placed the certificate in the coffin, where it will be with his body until the day of the resurrection.

That story illustrates many things, not least that there is hope for all of us. It also tells us that coming to Christ is a matter of the heart reaching out in faith to the Lord, not simply reciting some words or going through a religious ritual. Jim Johnsen found out that it's never too late to come to Christ. And you don't need a certificate to be certain that you will go to heaven when you die. The few words we wrote on that piece of paper simply summarized the message of this book. You don't need a certificate to go to heaven, but you do need to put your trust in Jesus Christ and Him alone.

The gospel is God's answer for those who aren't ashamed to admit they need help. If that is true, why do some people wait so long to come to Jesus? One man told me that many people wait because "they haven't hit bottom yet." Certainly many people feel self-sufficient and think they don't need the Lord. One can only pray that when they do hit bottom, they will finally look up and cry out for help. Putting things off keeps many people from God. We always think there is more time to decide. But life is so uncertain. "Do not boast about tomorrow, for you do not know what a day may bring forth" (Proverbs 27:1). One moment you are on top of the world; the next moment your plane crashes and your earthly life is over.

There comes a time when you must decide where you stand with Jesus. No one can sit on the fence forever. Not to decide is a decision in itself. If you don't say yes to Christ, you are actually saying no. To borrow a phrase from the great twentieth-century preacher Billy Graham, there is an "hour of decision" that comes to all of us sooner or later. I pray that this might be your hour to say yes to Jesus Christ.

The Gospel Made Plain

Since we are near the end of this book, let's take a moment to review what we've learned so far. I can summarize the whole gospel message in seven simple statements:

⇨ Admitting my need: To know the God who made me
⇨ Accepting God's judgment: Guilty as charged
⇨ Facing the truth: Helpless to save myself
⇨ Acknowledging God's solution: The Lord Jesus Christ
⇨ Remembering what He did: The cross and the empty tomb
⇨ Transferring your trust: From self to Christ alone

⇨Receiving eternal salvation: His righteousness for my sin

If you understand what those phrases mean, you know everything you need to know to go to heaven. The gospel begins with the God who made us. Although we were made to know Him, sin has separated us from Him. Because of sin we are truly guilty in God's eyes and left in a helpless condition, unable to save ourselves. Apart from divine grace we will die in our sins. If God doesn't do something, we're lost forever. The good news of the gospel is that God did something. He sent His Son, the Lord Jesus Christ, who perfectly fulfilled God's will and perfectly obeyed God's law. He succeeded where all of us failed so miserably. When He died, He died not for Himself (for He was sinless), but in our place, as a condemned man, bearing our sin and taking our punishment. What we deserved He took in our place. He made good on all His claims by rising from the dead on the third day. Salvation is offered to one and all on the condition that we turn from self-trust and self-confidence to trust wholly and completely in Christ alone. When we trust Christ in that fashion, God credits the righteousness of

Christ to us, and the penalty for our sin is paid in full. Thus we receive the benefit of what Christ accomplished two thousand years ago. This is the gospel of Jesus Christ.

The Bible uses a number of words and phrases to describe what happens to us when we wholeheartedly trust in Christ as Lord and Savior. We are forgiven, saved, born again, declared righteous in God's sight, given new life, pardoned, set free from the penalty of sin, brought into a new relationship with God, called a child of God, and assured of going to heaven when we die. This is "total salvation." It's free to us, but it's not cheap. It cost God the death of His one-and-only Son. The most famous verse in the Bible summarizes the message of this book in one simple yet profound sentence: **"For God so loved the world that he gave his one and only Son, that whoever believes in him shall not perish but have eternal life"** (John 3:16).

Salvation is available to anyone and everyone who wants it. God's offer is now on the table. What will you do with it?

Salvation Made Simple

A friend sent me an e-mail telling about a question asked by a coworker:

How is a Christian defined? It used to be that if you were not Jewish or Hindu or Buddhist, you were a Christian, whether Catholic or Lutheran or Episcopal or Baptist. But it seems now that the word means something more specific. Is it considered to be an actual religion other than Catholic or Lutheran or Episcopal or Baptist or whatever? If so, what makes it different?

That's a very good question. It shows that the person has been doing some serious thinking about spiritual issues. It also reveals that she has penetrated to a core issue that has long confused millions of people: What is the difference between being a Christian and a church member? The simplest way to answer that question is to say that a Christian is a person who has come to know God deeply and personally through a genuine saving faith in the Lord Jesus Christ. To say it that way means that while nearly all Christians are church members, not all church members are necessarily true Christians. Knowing God through Christ is about a personal relationship made possible through faith; it is not about religious ritual or merely "joining a church."

That truth leads us to an important point: No one "drifts" into Christianity by accident. At some point you must consciously trust Christ as Lord and Savior. In the words of nineteenth-century British pastor Charles Spurgeon, "You will never go to heaven in a crowd." It's true there will be crowds in heaven, but we only go there one at a time. God saves individuals, not masses or groups.

John 1:12–13 offers a simple outline of what it means to come to Christ for salvation: "Yet to all who received him, to those who believed in his name, he gave the right to become children of God—children born not of natural descent, nor of human decision or a husband's will, but born of God."

A Simple Step— Receiving Him

"To all who received him." The way of salvation begins with a simple step: *Receiving Christ as Lord and Savior.* The word "receive" means to welcome a visitor into your home. It's what happens when someone knocks at your door and you open the door and invite them to come in. To receive Christ means to welcome Him as an honored guest and to have Him make your heart His home.

A Wonderful Result— Child of God

"He gave the right to become children of God." The word "right" means "honor" or "privilege." The moment you receive Christ into your life, God gives you the honor of becoming a member of His family. This teaches us that not everyone is a child of God. All are created by God, but not everyone in the world is a child of God. Sometimes people carelessly say, "We're all God's children," but the Bible says no such thing. God only gives the privilege of being His children to those who by personal faith receive Jesus as Lord and Savior (Galatians 3:26).

That leads to some questions you ought to ask yourself:

"Not everyone is a child of God. Am I?"
"Not everyone has eternal life. Do I?"
"Not everyone will go to heaven. Will I?"

A Mysterious Truth— Born of God

"Children born not of natural descent, nor of human decision or a husband's will, but born of God." (John 1:13). This verse teaches us that God's grace doesn't run automatically from one generation to another. You aren't a Christian just because your parents were Christians or because your grandfather was an Episcopal bishop or your uncle a Baptist deacon. And you won't get brownie points with God just because you come from a good family and have a fine education. You can't save yourself by human effort, so don't bother trying. The sooner you stop trying to save yourself, the sooner you can be saved by God.

The whole gospel is contained in the little phrase "born of God." Salvation is of the Lord. *It's a free gift—totally free and totally of grace.* It's not a cooperative venture where you do your part and God does His. But someone may object, "Don't I have a part to play in salvation?" You do indeed have a part. Your part is to be hopelessly lost in sin. God's part is to save you. That way God alone gets the credit. Salvation is a work of God from first to last.

Time for a Decision

Sometimes we describe people who can't make a decision as being "on the fence." That perfectly describes the way many people relate to Jesus Christ. They want to know Him, they know they need Him, they truly feel their sin and want to find forgiveness, and perhaps they've even "decided to jump." But until they jump, they are still on the fence regarding Jesus. To use a biblical term, they are still lost.

To decide to receive Christ is good. Receiving Him by faith is much better.

Two thousand years ago Pontius Pilate, the Roman governor in Jerusalem, asked the crowd, "What do you want me to do with Jesus?" "Crucify Him!" they cried out. He asked the question because he wanted to shift responsibility for the decision away from himself. That never works. In the end each of us must decide what we will personally do with Jesus.

Curiosity is good if it leads you to the truth. Endless argument can be a way of avoiding the truth. In the end truth demands a personal commitment. You can talk about it, discuss it, debate it, and dissect it, but eventually you've got to do something about it. From God's point of view, believing in Christ is both an invitation and a command. In light of all that Christ has done, we are invited to trust Him as Lord and Savior. But this is not merely an option we can take or leave as if we might find a better offer somewhere else. To say that God commands us to believe in Christ means that if we refuse His offer of eternal life we will regret our wrong decision for all eternity. According to the Bible, the sin of unbelief is the greatest of all sins. Those who do not believe in Jesus are under God's wrath already. This solemn truth should make us stop and think carefully. Great issues are at stake. We must not trifle with the gospel.

The Old Testament contains a fascinating story about poisonous snakes sent by God to the people of Israel as a judgment on their sin (Numbers 21:5–9). When the people cried out for mercy, God told Moses to affix a bronze snake to a pole and place it where all the people could see it. Then they were told to look at the snake on the pole, and they would be spared. Look and live. Such a simple action, yet with such enormous consequences. John 3:14–15 applies that story to the work of Jesus Christ. Just as the bronze snake was lifted up in the wilderness, even so Jesus was "lifted up" on the cross to die for our sins. The invitation from God is the same. Look and live! Look in faith to Jesus and you will have eternal life. If you refuse to look, you will die. If you look, you will live.

Risking Eternity on Jesus

Ponder the words of this little verse:

Upon a life I did not live,
Upon a death I did not die,
I risk my whole eternity.

The "life I did not live" is the life of Jesus and the "death I did not die" is His death on the cross. When we trust Christ, we are "risking eternity" on Him. That is what it means to be a Christian. It means trusting in Christ so much that you risk your eternity on what He did for you in His life and in His death. I have sometimes told people that trusting Jesus for salvation means to trust Him so completely that if He can't take you to heaven, you aren't going to go there. Are you willing and ready to do that?

Perhaps it will help you to form your words into a very simple prayer. Even while I encourage you to pray this prayer, I caution you that saying words alone will not save you. Prayer doesn't save. Only Christ can save. But prayer can be a means of reaching out to the Lord in true saving faith. If you pray these words in faith, Christ will save you. You can be sure of that.

Lord Jesus, for too long I've kept You out of my life. I know that I am a sinner and that

I cannot save myself. No longer will I close the door when I hear You knocking. By faith I gratefully receive Your gift of salvation. I am ready to trust You as my Lord and Savior. Thank You, Lord Jesus, for coming to earth. I believe You are the Son of God who died on the cross for my sins and rose from the dead on the third day. Thank You for bearing my sins and giving me the gift of eternal life. I believe Your words are true. Come into my heart, Lord Jesus, and be my Savior. Amen.

If you have prayed this prayer in sincere faith, you may want to put your initials by the prayer along with today's date as a reminder that you have come to Christ in faith, trusting Him as your Lord and Savior.

In the end, I can't believe for you or you for me. Jesus said, "Come to me, all you who are weary and burdened, and I will give you rest" (Matthew 11:28). Will you come? Come and see for yourself. Come and discover how Christ can change your life.

If you are fearful, put your heart at ease. He avoids no seeker. He will not turn you away. God invites you. But still you must come. Do not hesitate. Stop making excuses. Come to Christ and be saved. Trust in Him and your new life will begin. Christ has opened the door and paid the price of admission in His own blood. Will you not trust Him and make Him your own? Christ has paid it all. He stands knocking at the door. What will your answer be?

Just As I Am

In 1822 a young woman named Charlotte Elliott was visiting some friends in the West End of London and there met a noted minister named César Malan. Over supper he asked her if she was a Christian. When she replied that she did not want to talk about the subject, the minister replied, "I did not mean to offend you. But I want you to know that Jesus can save you if you will turn to Him." Several weeks later they met again and Miss Elliott said that she had been trying to come to Christ but did not know how to do it. "Just come to Him as you are," Dr. Milan said. Taking the advice to heart, she composed a poem that began this way.

Just as I am, without one plea
but that Thy blood was shed for me,
And that Thou bidd'st me come to Thee,
O Lamb of God, I come, I come!

In 1849 William Bradbury set the words to music. Since then it has become one of the most beloved hymns of all time. For many years, Billy Graham has ended all his crusade sermons with the singing of "Just as I Am." The third verse contains Charlotte Elliott's own testimony:

Just as I am, though tossed about,
with many a conflict, many a doubt.
Fightings and fears within, without,
O Lamb of God, I come, I come!

And the last verse contains the gospel promise:

Just as I am, Thou wilt receive,
wilt welcome, pardon, cleanse, relieve;
Because Thy promise I believe,
O Lamb of God, I come, I come!

That is also the promise God makes to you and to me. If you will come—just as you are—and if you will believe the gospel promises, He will welcome, pardon, cleanse, relieve. May that be your experience as you come by faith to Jesus Christ, the great Lamb of God.

A TRUTH TO REMEMBER

We are invited to trust Christ as Lord and Savior. But this is not merely an option we can take or leave as if we might find a better offer somewhere else.

Going Deeper

Why do so many people confuse being a Christian with being a member of a Christian church? What's the essential difference between a real Christian and a religious person?

Why is it necessary to trust Christ personally?

Read John 3:1–7. Jesus said to Nicodemus, "You must be _____ again." What does that statement mean?

According to Jesus in John 6:47, what do you have through believing in Him?

Before going on, take time to read John 1:12–13 out loud. In order to make this powerful passage a part of your life, why not take time to memorize it?

9

FIRST STEPS IN a New Direction

TRUSTING CHRIST AS SAVIOR and Lord is the most important decision you will ever make. Your eternal destiny has been changed because of what Christ has done for you. But that is not the end of the story. In many ways, it is only the beginning.

Perhaps you have heard the term "born again" and wondered where it comes from. Originally, the term came from the lips of Jesus (John 3:3). It describes the new life He gives to those who come to Him in saving faith. Just as physical birth ushers in a new life that leads to physical growth, being born again spiritually produces in you a brand-new life that leads to spiritual growth.

Salvation in the biblical sense has three parts. First, you are saved from the guilt of sin in your past the moment you trust the Lord Jesus Christ. Second, you are being saved moment by moment from the power of sin in the present as you depend on the Lord and obey His commands. Third, you will be saved from the presence of sin in the future when you finally stand before the Lord in heaven. In that day, sin and its corrosive consequences will be removed from your life once and for all. While it is true that believers enjoy salvation now, the best is yet to come. We can see the three "tenses" of salvation very clearly in John 5:24, "I tell you the truth, whoever hears my word and believes him who sent me has eternal life and will not be condemned; he has crossed over from death to life." The believer "has crossed over" (that's the past), "has eternal life" (that's the present), and "will not be condemned" (that's the future).

I began this book by promising you some good news that could change your life. Part of the good news is that once you trust Christ, your sins are forgiven, Christ comes into your life, you become a part of God's family, and you receive the gift of eternal life. You don't need to fear death, for when you die, you will go to heaven to be with the Lord Jesus forever.

At the end of a conference in Hudson, Florida, an older couple drove me to the Tampa airport so I could catch my flight back to Chicago. As we talked, the father shared a tragic story about the death of one of his sons at the age of thirty-three. It happened just as the son was completing his training to be a missionary. Cancer took him in death after only three months. Before he died, he encouraged his parents with these words, "Don't worry about me. I'm just being transferred to Headquarters." His parents have cherished those words ever since his death.

Where does that faith come from? What hope do any of us have of going to heaven? Surely it is this: Through faith we have been united with Jesus Christ. When we die, we will be where Christ is, and we know where He is because forty days after He rose from the dead, the Lord Jesus Christ ascended into heaven (Acts 1:9–11). At the moment of death, the children of God can rest assured that the Christ who ascended bodily into heaven will take them to be with Him—and will one day raise their bodies immortal and incorruptible. "We know that God, who raised the Lord Jesus, will also raise us with Jesus and present us to himself together with you" (2 Corinthians 4:14 NLT). This assurance is not just for a selected few believers, but it is meant for all those who come to Christ in genuine saving faith.

Another part of the good news is that Christ comes into your life to change it from the inside out. As He makes Himself at home in your heart, you will discover new desires you never had before and new strength to empower your new desires. Second Corinthians 5:17 says that "if anyone is in Christ, he is a new creation; the old has gone, the new has come!" The Christian life begins the moment you trust Christ, but it doesn't end there. It continues day by day as you learn to walk with God, to grow in faith and love, to pray to your heavenly Father, to follow Jesus wherever He leads you, and to share His love with those you meet. If the Christian life is a book, coming to Christ is only chapter 1.

Here are some practical tips that will help you along the way.

Personal Assurance

• Don't base your salvation upon how you feel at a given moment. Even the greatest Christians have times of doubt and uncertainty. Doubt can even be good if it leads you back to a new confidence in God and in His Word.

- Don't base your salvation on an experience or even on your own faith. Remember that faith itself is a gift of God (Ephesians 2:8). You are not saved by faith in Christ but by Christ who saves you through faith. Rest your hope on who Jesus is and what He accomplished for you in His death and resurrection.

- Since salvation is of the Lord, you don't need to base your relationship with Christ on a date or a time when you had a certain experience. You don't consciously remember the moment of your birth, but you know you are alive. You may not remember the precise moment of your spiritual birth into God's family, but the Holy Spirit will give you assurance as you continue to believe God's promises and trust Christ alone as your Savior. First John 5:13 says clearly that you can know that you have eternal life. "I have written this to you who believe in the name of the Son of God, so that you may know you have eternal life" (NLT).

Spiritual Growth

- Just as physical growth happens slowly over time, the same is true in the spiritual arena. If you have struggled in some area before coming to Christ, it is altogether likely that you may continue to struggle in that area for some time to come. Pray about your problems. Find some other Christians to encourage you along the way. Be honest with the Lord about areas of your life that aren't changing as fast you would like. Use your struggles as an opportunity to grow.

- Jesus calls His followers disciples, which means "learners." Ask God every morning to help you follow Jesus all day long. Jesus also calls you to "take up your cross" daily, which means setting aside your own agenda to follow Christ (Luke 9:23–24).

- You will discover His agenda for your life through regular prayer, study of the Bible, by meditating on and memorizing key Scripture verses, and through the counsel of other Christian believers. All these things are part of the leading of the Holy Spirit, who now indwells you (1 Corinthians 6:19–20).

The Church

- One evidence of new life is that God gives you a love for other Christians (Ephesians 1:18). You certainly will grow much faster if you unite with a Bible-believing local church where the gospel is preached and Christians are challenged to serve the Lord. God never intended His children to be loners, living in cocoons, separated from each other. "We are all members of one body" (Ephesians 4:25). You need to be part of a local church for shared worship, following Christ in baptism, the regular experience of the Lord's Supper, fellowship with other Christians, and the opportunity to learn by listening to the teaching and preaching of God's Word. You also need the spiritual discipline of following godly leaders who can help you discover and use your spiritual gifts.

- God's heart embraces the whole world. Being part of a local church connects you to the worldwide Christian community. Through your church you will support missionaries in other countries and you will also learn of opportunities to unite with Christians in other churches in larger projects for the kingdom of God. The world notices when Christians truly love one another. Jesus said, "By this all people will know that you are my disciples, if you have love for one another" (John 13:35).

Spiritual Disciplines

- God gives His children a love for His Word. If you don't have a Bible, purchase one and begin to read it every day. Start with one of the Gospels (the book of Mark, for instance) and read the unfolding story of the life of Christ. Then make it a habit to read at least one psalm each day and also one chapter from the book of Proverbs.

- Most new believers discover that they gain much from being with a small group of believers on a regular basis. "Encourage each other and build each other up" (1 Thessalonians 5:11 NLT). Here you develop friendships, find a place to get your questions answered, and share stories of how God is helping each of you day by day. Most local churches make some provision for this kind of ministry, either through classes on Sunday or through groups that meet in homes during the week.

- Today there is a wealth of resources available to help you grow. These include various translations of the Bible, study Bibles with notes, books that help you understand the Bible and the Christian life, and an abundance of Christian music. In addition, there are computer programs and Internet sites filled with useful information. You may want to ask your pastor or your chaplain for some suggestions. If you don't know where to begin, visit a Christian bookstore near you and ask one of the staff to help you find some of these resources. Your church may have a lending library; this will also be a helpful source of books and tapes regarding Christian growth and Christian theology.

- Be sure to give God the first few minutes of every day. "In the morning, O Lord, you hear my voice; in the morning I lay my requests before you and wait in expectation" (Psalm 5:3). Take time to focus your heart and your thoughts on the Lord. You can do this through prayer, Bible reading, listening to good Christian music, and also by reading good devotional material that points you to the Lord and to His Word. The first few minutes are vital because they set the tone for the rest of the day. I suggest you keep a spiritual journal in which you write down key insights from Scripture and record the spiritual lessons the Lord teaches you through the circumstances of life.

- As you grow in Christ, you will find a new desire to share your material resources with others. Become a joyful giver. And how do you do that? By giving what you have to God. This certainly involves giving a portion of your money to the Lord through His church. You will also find many opportunities to give to those less fortunate than you. God loves a cheerful giver, but you can never experience that until you give joyfully from the heart.

Temptation and Sin

- Before too long you are certain to face temptation to sin. It will probably come at a moment when you don't expect it. Remember that temptation itself isn't a sin; it's how you respond that makes a difference. Whenever God allows you to be tempted, He also makes a way of escape (1 Corinthians 10:13). Pray for wisdom to see the way out and then ask God for courage to take that way when you see it.

- As you grow in your new life, the Holy Spirit will give you a desire to obey God and a growing hatred for sin. When you sin, you only have two choices. You can hide your sin and pretend it didn't happen, but if you do that, your life is certain to get worse, not better. Or you can confess your sin—admit what you did and ask God to forgive you. God blesses those people who confess their sins and ask for forgiveness. "If we confess our sins, he is faithful and just and will forgive us our sins and purify us from all unrighteousness" (1 John 1:9). He will give you both the desire and the power to say no to sin as you rely on Him.

Your Personal Witness

- It is natural for you to share your faith with others. Be bold in your faith (Acts 4:31). Don't let opposition silence your voice. Speak up for what you know is right. You may someday have to speak out against evil. Speak the truth in love and then trust God for the results. Your courage will bring you much joy and will encourage other Christians to be bold as well.

- Pray for opportunities to share the good news—the gospel—with others. Ask God to make you sensitive to those you meet each day. There are many ways to talk about Christ with someone else. Here's a simple

171

question that opens many doors: "How can I pray for you?" You might want to buy an extra copy of this book and have it on hand so that you can give it to a friend. Ask your friend to read it and tell you what he or she thinks about it.

• Coming to Christ changes the way you look at the world. Those who follow Jesus are called to be His ambassadors in the world— doing justice, loving mercy, and helping those in need. Ask God each day to help you make a difference in the world. Small things done in Jesus' name can have a huge impact on others.

Your Attitudes

• Asking questions is a great way to grow spiritually. As you study the Bible and as you listen to sermons and Bible studies, jot down your questions. See if you can find the answers on your own through your own personal study. If not, ask a friend or a trusted Christian leader to help you find the answers. Never be ashamed to admit you don't know something. That's always the first step in personal growth.

• Don't be surprised when hard times come. Jesus promised that in this world His followers would encounter much difficulty (John 16:33). God allows hard times to come in order to develop our faith, purify our motives, reorient our focus away from the things of the world, and enable us to grow spiritually. "Consider it pure joy, my brothers, whenever you face trials of many kinds, because you know that the testing of your faith develops perseverance" (James 1:2–3).When those hard times come, pray for endurance so that your faith will not fail.

- Gratitude is another mark that you are a child of God. All that you have, including life itself, comes from God. Take time daily to say "Thank You" to God for all His blessings. "Give thanks in all circumstances, for this is God's will for you in Christ Jesus" (1 Thessalonians 5:18). This will keep you from becoming hard and bitter when things don't go your way.

God's Plan for You

- Look for a chance to serve the Lord in some practical way. You will discover that God has given you talents that will enable you to serve the body of Christ, His church. As you serve, you will find great fulfillment and deep joy in the Lord. Don't limit yourself to what you think you would like to do. Ask God to use you in the way He deems best.

• Remember that coming to Christ is not like taking up a new hobby. It's the beginning of a new life where you come to know the God who created you. Although you don't realize it now, God has started a lifetime project of making you like His Son, the Lord Jesus Christ (Romans 8:29). You aren't a finished product yet, which is one reason why the Christian life won't always be easy.

Becoming a Christian means taking a journey that starts on earth and ends in heaven. If you have gotten this far in the book, I believe you are well on your way in your journey with the Lord. Keep on moving forward, keep your eyes on the prize, and you will not be disappointed. "Grow in the grace and knowledge of our Lord and Savior Jesus Christ" (2 Peter 3:18). In the spiritual life, direction makes all the difference. God is more interested in direction than perfection. Now that you have committed your life to Christ, there will be many surprises, some wonderful answers to prayer, and no doubt some major battles to fight. You may find yourself going up and down in your

Christian life. If that happens, don't despair. Just keep on moving forward with Christ. Daily obedience is the key. The Holy Spirit will help you to obey the Lord.

Some days you may feel as if you aren't making any progress at all. Don't let your feelings rule your life. Trust God and keep walking in the right direction.

With that we come to the end of this book. If you haven't yet trusted Christ as Savior and Lord, I encourage you to go back and read chapter 8 ("Coming to Christ") again. The gift of God is eternal life through Jesus Christ our Lord. The gift is yours for the taking. This is the good news that can change your life.

If God gives us understanding of who Jesus is and what He did for us, our only response can be to come to Him in love and trust, asking Him to save us. May God grant you faith to believe in Jesus Christ. If you have doubts, come and see for yourself. The way to heaven has been opened by the Son of God. Come just as you are, holding nothing back, making no excuses. Come, and as you come to Christ, He will come to you.

A TRUTH TO REMEMBER

Coming to Christ by faith is a lifetime journey that starts on earth and ends in heaven.

A Quick Review

Let's review what we've learned together. Listed below are a number of summary statements. Put a checkmark by each statement if you agree with it.

☐ God is infinite, eternal, holy, righteous, all-knowing, all-powerful. He created me in His image.

☐ God loves me and wants to have a relationship with me.

☐ I was made to know God personally.

☐ I am a sinner.

First Steps in a New Direction

☐ My sins separate me from God.

☐ I am truly guilty and unable to save myself.

☐ I can never be good enough to save myself.

☐ God sent His Son, Jesus Christ, to be my Savior.

☐ Jesus died on the cross for my sins.

☐ Jesus rose from the dead on the third day.

☐ I am not saved by what I do but by what Christ has done for me.

☐ When I trust Christ, He takes my sin and I receive the gift of His righteousness.

☐ Salvation is a free gift offered to anyone who trusts Christ as Savior.

☐ I am trusting Jesus Christ as my Lord and my Savior.

Go back and read the prayer on pages 155–56. If you are truly trusting Christ, put your initials and today's date by that prayer.

Going Deeper

What are the next steps you need to take on your spiritual journey?

If you have just trusted Christ as Savior, who else needs to know about your decision?

A SEVEN-DAY PLAN
for Spiritual Growth

Day 1: Read John 3. Circle every instance of the word "believe" or "believes."

Day 2: Tell a friend about your decision to trust Christ as Savior.

Day 3: Spend time today praying for spiritual guidance.

Day 4: Memorize Philippians 4:13. Share it with a friend.

Day 5: Ask God to lead you to someone who needs a word of encouragement.

Day 6: Meditate on Psalm I. Write it down word for word and then say it out loud.

Day 7: Find a church where the Bible is taught. Attend worship services this Sunday.

Acknowledgments

I OWE A DEBT of gratitude to a number of friends who read the manuscript and made many helpful comments:

First Edition (2000): John Armstrong, Brian Bill, Jeff Eaton, Rob Gaskill, Seth Grotelueschen, Chris Jahns, Lisa King, Dale Stoffer.

Second Edition (2011): Jessica Harris, Don Johnson, Skip Olson, Tim Plona, Adrienne Urbanski.

RAY PRITCHARD serves as president of Keep Believing Ministries, an Internet-based community serving Christians in 220 countries. He served in the pastorate for twenty-six years, most recently at Calvary Memorial Church in Oak Park, Illinois. Dr. Pritchard is the author of twenty-seven books, including *Stealth Attack*, *The Incredible Journey of Faith*, *The Healing Power of Forgiveness*, and *Names of the Holy Spirit*. Ray and Marlene have been married for thirty-six years. They have three sons and two daughters-in-law and one grandson. All of their sons and daughters-in-law have spent time in recent years teaching English in China. Three of Dr. Pritchard's books have been translated into Chinese. He enjoys the Internet, riding his bike, and anything related to the Civil War.

If you would like to contact the author, you can reach him in the following ways:

By mail: Ray Pritchard
              Keep Believing Ministries
              P. O. Box 257
              Elmhurst, IL 60126

By e-mail: Ray@KeepBelieving.com
Via the Internet: www.KeepBelieving.com

Beyond All You Could Ask or Think

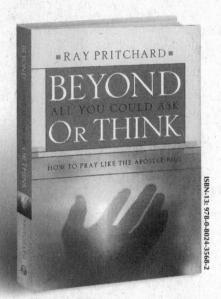

If we truly believed in a powerful, all-knowing, all-loving God, would we not take every large and small concern to Him? Dr. Ray Pritchard writes in a popular style that will compel you to make prayer a consistent and disciplined practice.

MOODY
PUBLISHERS

www.MoodyPublishers.com

Names of the Holy Spirit

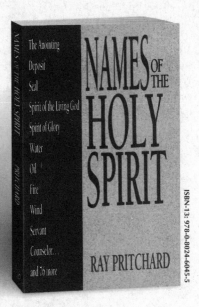

His Power. His indwelling. His anointing.
His gifts. This book provides a deeper
understanding of the Person and works of
the third member of the Holy Trinity.

www.MoodyPublishers.com

STEALTH ATTACK

Ray Pritchard tackles spiritual terrorism in
Stealth Attack. By drawing upon the teaching
and examples of Jesus, Peter, Paul, and others,
he offers practical steps for outmaneuvering the
most shameless and stealthy foe imaginable.

www.MoodyPublishers.com